W9-BCO-549

AN IRISH
CHRISTMAS

AN IRISH CHRISTMAS

JOHN B. KEANE

CARROLL & GRAF PUBLISHERS, INC.
NEW YORK

Copyright © 1999 by John B. Keane

All rights reserved.

First Carroll & Graf edition 2000

Carroll & Graf Publishers, Inc.
A Division of Avalon Publishing Group
19 West 21st Street
New York, NY 10010-6805

Library of Congress Cataloging-in-Publication Data is available.
ISBN: 0-7867-0815-8

Manufactured in the United States of America

CONTENTS

The Fourth Wise Man

Canon Coodle sighed happily. It was Christmas. He had just finished hearing confessions and to clear his head from the fog of sin, or what his parishioners believed to be sin, he had decided upon a walk around the church grounds which were as extensive as any you'd find in the country. His thoughts turned heavenward as they always did after a session in the confessional. He would have liked a glass of vintage port but it was still bright. He looked at his watch and came to the conclusion that darkness was imminent. Perhaps when the dusk surrendered its diminishing claims to daylight he would indulge, just one glass, no more. Before retiring that night he would consume two final glasses and then graciously surrender himself to the arms of Morpheus. Canon Coodle had spent eighty-two Christmases in the world but had never really felt the burden of his years. 'I'll die in harness,' he informed his physician, 'because I would hate to end up as a problem for someone.'

'Oh you'll die in harness all right,' Dr Matt Coumer assured him a few weeks earlier when the canon had called to the surgery for his bi-annual overhaul.

'Is there something wrong?' the canon asked matter-of-factly as though it did not concern him.

'Your blood pressure's up and your heart is tricky. I can think of no other word for that particular heart of yours. Apart from the fact that you should have been dead years ago there's little else the matter.' Dr Coumer put aside his stethoscope and indicated to his parish priest that they should both be seated. 'You have only one problem canon,' the doctor leaned back in his chair and looked his elderly patient in the eye.

'And pray what would that be?'

'Two days hence on St Stephen's day you will have bands of wrenboys calling to the presbytery as they have been doing since you first came here. Your predecessors cleared them from the presbytery door for all the wrong reasons. You changed all that and we admire you for it but in one way you might be better off if the wrenboys stayed away from your door too.'

'Never!' Canon Coodle rose from his chair.

'Please sit down,' Matt Coumer spoke in the gentlest of tones as if he were reproving a wayward child. The canon sat and listened.

'In the past you have been known to dance jigs and hornpipes with each of the bands on the steps leading up to the presbytery door. All I'm asking you to do my dear friend is to dance with only one band on this occasion. If you do as I ask there's a good chance you'll see one more Christmas at least. If you persist in dancing with all the bands you'll be in danger of a seizure. Promise me now like a good man,' Dr Coumer reverted to the gentle tones he had used earlier, 'that all you'll dance on St Stephen's day is one hornpipe and one reel. Promise.'

'I promise,' Canon Coodle forced out the words against his will. He rose and shook hands with his physician who, in turn, placed a protective arm around the old man's shoulder.

As the canon recalled his visit he regretted the

promise he had made. Round and round the church grounds he walked as if he were competing in a race. 'Promises were made to be broken', he recalled the saying and then he smashed the fist of his right hand into the palm of his left 'but not by Canon Cornelius Coodle' he concluded in triumph with the voice of a man who had never broken a promise.

He decided to return to the warmth of the presbytery sitting-room and therein to partake of his ration of port as he termed the measure. Later there would be the Christmas Eve Masses and later still there would be a Christmas drink or two with his curates and two of the most amiable chaps imaginable he considered them to be. They would tease him of course about the flawed full forward line of the Ballybo Gaelic football team. The canon had first seen the light in Ballybo 'and is he proud of it!' the curates would tell their families when asked what sort of priest was Canon Coodle.

When they finished with Ballybo they would start about Celtic and their run in the Scottish League. The canon's first curacy had been in Glasgow. He would be a Celtic fan till the man above blew the whistle and called him from the field of play. He always favoured a melodramatic turn of phrase when arguing football with curates. It was what they expected of him and he would never let them down.

As the trio savoured their drinks in the brightly lit sitting-room they were joined by Mrs Hanlon, the housekeeper, who drank not at all but who, the curates suspected, would play her customary role of timekeeper as the clock ticked merrily on towards twelve. On Christmas night and New Year's eve, of all the nights of the year, she would stand benignly by, as Canon Coodle put it, and suffer silently the yearly massacres of *Danny Boy* and *The Last Rose of Summer* as the canon also put it, by himself and his specially invited colleagues from parishes near and far.

She sat now silently and most reposefully while the sacred hour approached. It was her favourite time, a time to savour, above all other times, for the birth of Christ was at hand and downstairs in the kitchen her turkey was ready for the morning oven with bread stuffing and potato stuffing close by, with ham cooked and glazed, with giblet stock prepared for soup and gravy, with the primed fortified special trifle at the ready and the plum pudding waiting to be steamed. It could be said that her cup was running over. Her drowsy eyes blinked but barely when the glasses of her three charges clinked.

'It's the sort of night,' she reminded herself, 'when a drunk is bound to show up at the front door looking for the canon or one of the curates to drive him home. Only six miles. Couldn't get a taxi. Wife and kids at home with no one to fill the role of Santa. On the other hand it might be an even more drunken wretch looking for a priest to give the last rights to a mother who was far healthier than he was.'

As ill-luck would have it the presbytery's inmates would not be left in peace until the sacristan rang the warning bell well in advance of first Mass on the morning of Christmas Day. A surprise lay in store.

'Now lads!'

Mrs Hanlon raised first her head from near her lap to where it had drooped with the weight of drowsiness and secondly her body from the chair which was ever so narrowly withdrawn outside the priestly triangle round the fire.

Canon Coodle was reminding his listeners of the time his uncle, a country schoolmaster, had shared a public house counter for a short period with Hilaire Belloc while the latter had been visiting Dublin.

'The poor man,' the canon continued with a chuckle, 'never spoke about anything else for the rest of his life.' The canon suddenly rose, extended his right hand and quoted from his uncle's acquaintance:

> Dons admirable! Dons of might!
> Uprising on my inward sight
> Compact of ancient tales and port
> And sleep and learning of a sort.

As the trio rose the housekeeper faded into the darkest corner of the room from where she would emerge to see to the fire and lights after the priests' departure to their upstairs rooms. The canon led his curates to the foot of the stairs, both hands extended now as he quoted once more from Belloc:

> I will hold my house in the high wood
> Within a walk of the sea
> And the men who were boys when I was a boy
> Will sit and drink with me.

Before they exchanged goodnights the trio said that it was the gentlest night of Christmas ever spent by any of the three. They had, they felt, effortlessly introduced the real spirit of Christmas into their midst and prepared themselves for the feast day that was to come.

No sooner had Canon Coodle eased himself into his bed than the housekeeper appeared at the bedside after first knocking on the bedroom door. On a tray she bore his nightcap, a small measure of whiskey topped up with boiling water and flavoured with cloves and lemon. She waited till the very last drop was swallowed after which she drew the curtains and waited for the first low key-snore of the night.

As the canon slumbered so did he dream of his mother. She had passed on to her eternal reward shortly after his ordination. He was still young enough at the time to shed abundant tears for many months after her burial. Then with the passage of time as the grief melted into fond recall he could recall their times together without sorrow. She had once asked him, not long before his ordination, if there was a girl. He had shaken his head but of course there had been a girl. Hadn't that been the case always and wasn't it the case for many years thereafter but these were merely girls of the mind and with these phantom creatures all men must contend before sleep dulls the senses. Always the canon would spend his last waking moments thinking of his mother. Other nights he would dream of Gaelic football when he saw himself soaring above the heads of his opponents, reaching into the heavens where only the doughtiest and most agile of footballers soared in search of the pig-skin as it was known in country places in the days when Corny Coodle could out-field any man in the seven parishes. He was denied a place on the county team but only because his *alma mater*, Maynooth College, frowned upon high level commitment on the grounds that the sweet taste of physical glory might out-weigh the spiritual and the mystical. It happened all too often and it was believed by many that those who surrendered the spiritual to the physical turned their backs on the Roman collar and would always be deficient in outlook and aspiration.

'Hogwash!' was the only comment Canon Coodle would offer when such opinions were aired.

He would remember a classmate in his final year, one Tommy Henley who withdrew from the race within weeks of his ordination because of pressure to stay away from county football. He had played under a variety of assumed names but when the college authorities discovered this duplicity they determined that he would abide by the rules or withdraw. He had opted for the latter.

Canon Coodle fondly remembered Tommy's marriage to Maryanne Fogarty. It had been a joyous wedding and were there not now twelve Henleys from that glorious union, all doing well in the world and was not one of them ordained. Canon Coodle stirred in his sleep. He found himself tussling for a ball with a Corkman named Tyers. The ball eluded both at their first attempt but Coodle got a hand to it to stop it from going over the line and wide. It fell to Tyers to raise the ball into his grasp with his right foot and so it went on until blows were very nearly exchanged. It was precisely at that moment that the canon opened his eyes to find himself being manhandled by his junior curate.

'Wake, wake, for God's sake canon!' the curate cried out.

The canon sat upright in his bed wondering if he was playing host to an unwelcome dream.

'It's the crib canon!' the curate threw both hands

high in the air at the monstrosity of the entire business.

'What about the crib!' the canon asked calmly, 'is it on fire or what?'

'No, no, no!' the curate was screaming now. 'They are trying to wrest the boy scouts' box from the wall beside it.'

'But dang it!' the canon exclaimed disbelievingly, 'the boy scouts' box is part of the chapel wall.'

'Well they have a pick-axe and they have a hammer and chisel and they're hacking away like hell and they're drunk to boot.'

The canon had moved himself to the side of the bed where he sat momentarily.

'And where is the senior curate?' he asked.

'Fr Sinnott is on sick call,' he was informed by a now more composed junior curate.

'Where is Mrs Hanlon?' the canon asked fearfully.

'She's rung the civic guards,' he was at once informed, 'and now she's keeping an eye on the robbers till help comes.'

'Well help is at hand,' the canon raised his great voice and demanded his dressing-gown.

'Follow me!' he called. The canon would have been happier had the junior curate's role been reversed with that of his senior. He had seen Fr Sinnott on the football field, a tough customer who revelled in rough play and was not above planting the occasional consecrated wallop on the jaw of a would be blackguard.

'Ballybo forever!' Canon Coodle shouted out the war cry of his native place as his six feet two inches, fifteen stones and eighty-two years bore down upon the sacrilegious wretches who dared tamper with his boy scouts' box, a veritable treasure chest which was now held in the arms of an emaciated cut-throat on his way to the door which he had earlier broken in. He was followed by two henchmen armed with pick-axe, hammer and chisel.

'My strength is as the strength of ten', Canon Coodle issued the warning before crashing headlong into the wielder of the pick-axe. The wielder fell, wind-ed and semi-conscious. The bearer of the chisel and hammer was to suffer a worse fate for as soon as he intimated that he meant business he was struck to the floor and rendered unconscious by Fr Sinnott who had just entered via the sacristy. At that moment the canon challenged the gang's ringleader.

'Drop that box,' he warned, 'or suffer the conse-quences. By the double dang,' the canon went on as he raised himself to his full height, 'you're for an early grave sir unless you yield.'

Yield the scoundrel did but it was not because of the canon's command. Rather had his trusty house-keeper edged her way behind the ringleader and em-bedded her knitting needle in his unprotected poster-ior. He dropped the boy scouts' box as though it were a box of adders and ran screaming into the night, leaving his henchmen to the tender mercies of an enraged Fr Sinnott. When the civic guards arrived as they did almost immediately after they had been sum-moned their main worry was the containment of the senior curate. It proved to be no easy task for Fr Sinnott was as strong as the proverbial horse. After a while aided by the canon's mollifying tones and the house-keeper's tender words they managed to seat him in a pew. Then and only then did the junior curate appear. He had taken up his position in the crib, next to St Joseph from where he had hurled sacred candles at the invaders.

It transpired that the box held several hundred pounds. The civic guards took the money with them for safe-keeping as they did the leaderless rogues who would have denied the boy scouts the summer holiday which the generous subscriptions of the parishioners had guaranteed them

'Coodle is the truest boy scout of them all', the middle-aged sergeant of the civic guards announced to his two companions as they opened a bottle in the barracks to celebrate the capture. Later the ringleader would be happy to give himself up as the cold of the night proved itself to be the master of his mettle.

In the presbytery the triumphant foursome were content to re-occupy their warm beds and sleep the sleep of the blessed. Word of their exploits spread and would-be raiders gave the church and presbytery a wide berth from that sacred morning forward.

Christmas Day was a happy day as was the night that followed. The parishioners one and all commented over their Christmas dinners on the text of Canon Coodle's sermon. In it he had praised exceedingly the closeness of the family and the power of the family when beset by the force of evil. He was referring, of course, to the Holy Family of Jesus, Mary and Joseph but when he went on to suggest that all who shared the same roof were, in a sense, families too they knew that he was referring to the inmates of the presbytery and the role they had played in defending each other and their property when unity was needed.

In spite of this the younger curate was bestowed with a sobriquet which would stay with him even when he left the parish. He became known as the Fourth Wise Man. Nobody knew who was responsible for the nickname but almost everybody in the community was agreed that it was a wise move indeed to seek the sanctuary of the holy crib when confronted by hostile forces twice his size and armed to the teeth.

The achievements of the others guaranteed lasting veneration. The Fourth Wise Man went on to become a parish priest in the course of time and Fr Sinnott the senior curate ended up a monsignor. The occasion would be remembered as the night of the Fourth Wise Man.

As Christmas drew to a close Canon Coodle sat in the presbytery sitting-room with his housekeeper. 'If there is one sound,' he told her after he had sipped from his glass of port, 'that I love above all others it is the distant pulse of the bodhrán, the drum of drums, the native drum of Ireland. If tomorrow is as fine as the forecasters have promised we will be able to hear it from great distances.'

In the canon's study a sensitive goat-skin drum, beloved of wrenboys and stepdancers, hung from the ceiling to remind him of the days when, as a youngster, and indeed as a young man, he roved the countryside with his companions of the Ballybo Wrenboys Band under their captain the Tipper Coodle. The Tipper, uncle to the young Corny Coodle, was so called because of his preference for the bare knuckle over the cipín or wooden drumstick with a knob at either end.

Every band of the time would have an equal number of drummers and tippers, the tippers favouring the knuckle, the drummers favouring the cipín. Often the tippers would play even when the blood began to show on the backs of their bare hands such was their zeal in the pursuance of perfection.

'I tell you now with no word of a lie,' the canon confided to his housekeeper, 'those tippers could make the bodhráns talk and my dear uncle, God be good to him, could play and dance at the same time especially when he had a few whiskeys inside of him.'

'You're a fair dancer yourself canon,' Mrs Hanlon spoke out of a sense of appreciation rather than from a sense of duty as she recalled the canon's exploits at the front of the presbytery on previous St Stephen's days.

'He would dance with every group,' she informed her sister Bridgie whenever she visited the family home in the hills at the southern end of the parish, 'and out of his own pocket would come a ten pound note for every band. I remember when it was a ten shilling note but a ten shilling note then was as good as a tenner now.'

The money, of course, would go towards the purchase of drink and edibles for the annual wren dances, several of which would be held all over the parish until the month of January expired. The previous canon would have nothing to do with wrenboys, labelling them drunkards and scoundrels and turning them away from the presbytery door. In the end they bypassed the presbytery altogether but all changed dramatically when Canon Coodle was appointed as parish priest.

The canon's face darkened a little when he recalled the terpsichorean restrictions imposed upon him by his physician. Never downcast for long he raised his great head and smiled at the prospect of the two dances which had been permitted to him. He resolved to invest more concentration and commitment into these than ever before and, please God, he would have his fill of the dance before the day was out.

As they sat, the canon reminiscing, the housekeeper deftly used her knitting needles to complete the cardigan which she had undertaken to knit for her sister. The bright needles moved like lightning in her practised fingers, one of them the same needle which had perforated the vile rear of the robbers' ringleader. The wound inflicted needed medical attention and when Dr Coumer called to the barracks on the morning of St Stephen's Day to re-examine the sore he was able to tell Sergeant Ruttle that it would take several days to heal.

'You'll have a drink before you leave,' Sergeant Ruttle insisted.

'I have a call to make,' he said.

'It can't be that serious.' The sergeant took a bottle of whiskey from his desk.

'I assure you,' said Matt Coumer at his most emphatic, 'that it is likely to be the most important call I shall make this day.' So saying he closed his black bag and made straight for the presbytery where he was immediately shown into the august presence of his parish priest.

'You can leave your coat on canon,' he announced warmly, 'for I have not come to examine you.'

'And why have you come my dear Matt?' the canon asked solicitously.

'I have come,' Matt informed him, 'to restore your licence.'

'And pray what licence would that be?' the canon asked, a look of anxiety appearing on his face.

'Your dance licence of course my dear canon,' Matt informed him, 'you may dance as much as you please and if my ears don't deceive me I believe I hear the sound of bodhráns so get your dancing shoes on. I'll stay to watch and enjoy a drop of your whiskey while I do.'

A Christmas Come Uppance

Canon Cornelius Coodle heaved a great sigh and ran gaunt fingers through his heavily-silvered hair. At eighty-two he was still one of the more presentable priests in the diocese. Certainly he was the most distinguished-looking. When he spoke people listened. Nobody fell asleep during his sermons.

'Oh he calls a spade a spade sure enough,' the older farmers in the parish's hinterland were fond of saying, 'even if he does throw back a drop or two in excess now and then.'

'All he takes is a drop of port for God's sake,' the farmers' wives would respond defensively.

Removing his hands from his head Canon Coodle examined his smooth palms as though he might find in them a solution to the problem which had so recently been relayed to him on the phone. The voice at the other end had been that of his bishop.

'Bad news Corny,' the bishop had opened. He went on to inform his right arm, the name by which he always referred to the canon, of several distressing sightings of one Fr Tom Doddle, ecclesiastic-in-chief of Cooleentubber, a struggling parish in the easternmost part of the diocese. 'He was seen only last evening,' the bishop informed the right arm, 'vainly trying to negotiate a simple street corner. When a friendly civic guard came to his assistance he ranted and raved over the stupidity of an urban council which dared to place such abominable obstructions in the path of an innocent wayfarer.

'I tell you Corny,' the bishop continued, 'that if this insufferable staggering doesn't end at once we'll all be disgraced.'

'What can I do Pádraig?' Canon Coodle asked gently. Only the canon, at the bishop's behest, was permitted to address the diocesan leader by his Christian name.

'What I want you to do Corny is get him to go off the drink right away or, failing that, get him to reduce his intake – but most off all I want you to stop him staggering in public.'

There followed a silence. After a short interval the bishop resumed where he had left off. 'A staggering clergyman,' he told his canon, 'is a parody of the priesthood, a degradation of all we hold sacred, an abomination to the eye.'

While the bishop's litany continued Canon Coodle brought up to mind the only occasion he had ever staggered. He had been a green curate at the time. He had accompanied his parish priest Fr Willie Sidle to a Station Mass. After the celebration of the Mass both priests sat at a table, already partially manned by four local dignitaries, strong farmers all. After breakfast the talk turned to Gaelic football. The young curate was astonished at the inroads made into three bottles of Powers Gold Label as the morning matured into noon. For his part, after declaring his preference for port, he downed a mere half bottle. It was he who later guided the docile mare home while Fr Sidle issued a running commentary on the football prowess of the many farmers and labourers they encountered on their way back to the presbytery.

As they both untackled the mare from the parochial trap Fr Sidle paused in his labours in order to tender some advice to his curate. Earlier the parish priest had been surprised when the curate had indulged in a mild stagger as they departed the Station house.

'Observe!' he instructed his junior, 'my carriage and my disposition. I do not stagger under drink for two reasons. First I know to the drop what I can consume and secondly I would rather be hung like a dog before I would give it to say to any man that I am a staggerer. My drinking habits, as long as I don't show drink, are between me and my liver. I like football. I've seen you play Coodle and you're a decent half-back. I've seen you ship many a hard tackle but you never went down because you wouldn't give it to say that you were hurt. Go now and drink your moderate quota of port on occasion but stagger no more like a decent fellow.'

'Are you there Corny?' The bishop's exasperated tone brought Canon Coodle back to the time that was in it.

'You're not to worry,' the canon spoke with what he hoped was canonical assurance.

'That's good to hear Corny.' The bishop sounded mollified but he wasn't finished.

'Dang it,' he went on, 'I served under priests who could drink Lough Lein if they had the price of it but I never saw one of them stagger.'

The first thing Canon Coodle did after his bishop had hung up was to toast his late mentor Fr Willie

Sidle. Fr Sidle had been his model during those form-
ative early years.

'Fr Willie,' his parishioners boasted, 'always drinks
his nuff at weddings, wakes, Stations and the like but
he never drinks more than his nuff.'

Finishing his port the canon folded his once mighty
hands over his ample paunch and pondered his problem. Desperate ills he told himself require desperate
remedies and with this precept as his guide he began
to formulate his plan.

Now Cornelius Coodle was not an envious man but
if there was to be a momentary visitation from the
deadliest of the seven deadly sins the man he would
most envy would be Simon Tabley. Simon was a friend,
however, a close and trusted one as were most of the
teachers under the canon's management. Simon could
carry his liquor. He drank during weekends only.

'He drinks like a fish,' a local wag once told his
cronies, 'but the difference is that he don't make no
splash.'

What the wag said was true. Simon, a childless
widower in his late fifties, was principal of the Boys'
National School. His only interest in life after his video
camera, was his devotion to whiskey consumption
during weekends. His wife had been the victim of a
youthful speedster's erratic driving. Simon had been
lucky to survive and was in receipt of generous in-
surance. 'I would forfeit every penny,' he once confided to the canon, 'if I could hold her in my arms for
a minute, a single minute my dear friend.'

The canon had nodded, his ancient face flushed

by a port-induced rufescence. At the time Simon was quite taken by the angelic expression on the old man's face. A translation from the Gaelic came to him from memory:

As sacred candle
In a holy face
Such is the beauty
Of an ancient face.

When the pair met the following weekend Simon contained his curiosity as best he could. He had brought with him a bottle of vintage port and before he could sit down he found himself with a glass of whiskey in his hand. His entry to the canon's sitting-room coincided with that of the two curates.

'I'm off canon,' the senior curate informed his superior, 'you will be called, I hope, for ten o'clock Mass in the morning.'

'What a personable chap,' the schoolmaster commented after he had taken a tiny sip from his unwatered whiskey. The canon showed his gratification with a benevolent nod. He had, after all, taught his assistant most of what he knew.

'And the other one?' Simon asked.

'Excellent young man, a beer perhaps when he is off duty, nothing while he's on.'

The preliminaries over, Canon Coodle addressed his visitor. 'There is,' he began, 'in this very diocese a floundering philanderer of a clergyman who seems to be quite incapable of walking in an upright manner while under the influence of drink. In fact,' the canon continued sarcastically, much to his visitor's surprise, 'he inflicted his undesirable presence on this very parish quite recently and literally passed himself out with a variety of hitherto-unaccomplished staggers. In short my dear friend he disgraced himself on the streets of this very parish, my parish. I understand his house-keeper drives him here on a regular basis and when she's finished her shopping mercifully drives him off again. Apparently he presents a soberer mien at his own front door as it were.'

'How's he otherwise?' Simon asked.

'Otherwise,' the canon grudgingly conceded, 'he seems to be all right.'

Simon found himself somewhat perplexed. The canon seemed to be stepping out of character a little. It must be his aversion to staggering he told himself.

'How can I help?' he asked.

'You can help by making a short video of one of his performances when he next intrudes in my baili-wick.'

'I don't know that I can do that canon,' Simon informed his friend.

'Oh you can do it,' the canon assured him, 'you have no choice. You don't want to see the children of the parish scandalised. A clergyman staggering through the streets of this town is the last thing any of us wishes to see. Suppose it was a teacher?' the canon suggested.

Simon decided not to rise to this bait. He person-ally knew several teachers who staggered occasionally when under the influence and even if they weren't al-ways discreet about it Simon failed to see the harm in it unless it happened in the school or on the school grounds.

'Who would see this video?' he asked.

26

'Well,' the canon paused for a moment, 'there wouldn't be any point in the exercise if the star of the show didn't see it. I would see it and you would see it but nobody else. The idea is to show the poor wretch the error of his ways and then we'll destroy the evidence.'

'I'll do it because I know you mean well,' Simon agreed, 'although I have certain misgivings.'

'I'll never be able to repay you,' the canon gratefully replenished his friend's glass and returned to his armchair.

'Will it be difficult?' he asked.

'Shouldn't be,' Simon assured him, 'I know our quarry fairly well and I know his runs. Generally he arrives in town about three o'clock on Monday afternoons. I've spotted him on my way to the post office after school, calls to the hotel, to Brady's, O'Grady's, Mulligan's, Brannigan's and Crutley's, commences to stagger after leaving Brannigan's, shortish staggers really more like mis-steps until he emerges from Crutley's, his final port of call. Then the comprehensive staggers commence, be a piece of cake, nobody minds me on the streets, especially with my video. They're well used to me. I'll do the job and with average luck I'll have the finished product here on Monday night, a week before Christmas.'

'And I'll have my man here the following morning,' the canon promised.

The friends had another drink before parting, Canon Coodle to his bed and Simon to Brady's Bar or more precisely to the back lounge or inner sanctum of the widely revered premises. There he would sip until

Mrs Brady gently reminded her special customers that it was time to go home.

True to form Fr Tom Doddle, parish priest of Cooleentubber, erupted from the ornate doorway of Crutley's Bar on to the main street where he collided with several passers-by. He escaped any form of de-railment or injury himself. His victims were not so lucky. One young man who had been somewhat un-sighted in the first place was knocked to the ground. He arose, none the worse for his encounter, dazed and badly shaken, after a short while. On his feet he assumed a fighting stance and challenged the on-lookers to a fair fight. When no one took up his offer he wished all and sundry a Merry Christmas and sat on an adjacent window-sill in order to confirm his bearings.

As Fr Tom Doddle staggered onwards in ever-increasing lurches he was videoed front face, side face and rear by Simon until the schoolmaster was satisfied that he had captured a true portrait of the wayward cleric.

Time passed and at the appointed hour the film was set in motion by Simon. With mounting annoyance the canon followed the erratic progress of Fr Doddle. He cast a side glance now and then at his friend but that worthy merely sat with folded arms, expression-less and impassive.

'What's this?' Canon Coodle asked in alarm as his eyes returned to the small screen.

The question was followed by gasping sounds of disbelief and by various exclamations of astonish-ment. 'Oh no!' Canon Coodle covered his face with his hands. 'Can that awful parody really be me?' he asked, his voice broken, his face anguished.

'Have I seen myself as I really am Simon or is this video a distortion of my true self?'

'The video doesn't lie canon, not this time anyway. You've just seen yourself at a bad time and that can be unnerving.'

'Did you do this deliberately Simon because if you did I'm most grateful for giving me a look at the horrible old windbag I really am.'

'Not deliberately canon. You just happened to be in the vicinity.'

'But I look awful,' the canon cried out. 'I look drunk, trampish, farcical, infinitely worse than that poor priest.'

'No canon. You just look a bit weary that's all. You're no chicken you know.'

The canon raised his eyes aloft. He remembered the occasion clearly now. He had been on his way home from his pre-Christmas visit to the convent where his good friend the reverend mother had plied him with vintage port. He remembered saying to himself on his way home that he was a little unsteady on his feet but then he admitted 'I often am and I need not have a single port taken. I remember I had my hat in one hand and my walking stick in the other just like we saw there,' the canon laughed, happily now, 'and my scarce, grey locks blowing in the wind like Lear but he had only a crown whereas I have a Roman collar. I've seen the light Simon. I was fast becoming a whining, old hypocrite. I missed the mote in my own eye but I'll never make the same mistake again. I'm so grateful to you my boy. I wish you a happy, holy and wonderful Christmas and now will you please do something about our empty glasses so that I can celebrate my escape from hypocrisy.'

ANGELS IN OUR MIDST

Never pass an acquaintance or, indeed any man or woman, without conferring upon them that most inexpensive of all gifts – the common or garden salute. This applies especially at Christmas when people of all ages wish each other happy Christmases, holy Christmases and merry Christmases. Sometimes those with generous dispositions or with time on their hands also wish all and sundry a happy New Year. I believe this to be a commendable practice and I am glad that I find the opportunity in this collection of yuletide tales to indulge in my favourite eccentricity as my beloved wife sometimes calls it.

When we salute people, no matter how enlightened or well intentioned the sentiments, we must always be prepared for rebuff. When we wish other people happy Christmases we should try to realise that some are incapable of being happy because they enjoy being unhappy. Some enjoy being morose while others like to be churlish. I once had a distant cousin, now even more distant, God rest him since he expired in a fit of pique a few Christmases ago. He saw a group of people laughing hysterically on his way home from church and was overcome by disgust. Promptly he fell down and died poor fellow.

Another relation of mine, still with us, would faint upon beholding a radiant face and then there was a friend who never returned a salute. He would respond with grimaces and rude sounds. In case you are asking yourself why the preamble to this tale, if tale it can be called, I will not keep you waiting any longer. I am simply trying to ready the gentle reader for the unexpected.

On the most recent Christmas Eve at precisely twenty-five minutes past eleven I decided to go for a stroll through the streets of my native town. Before I left the house I underwent a wifely inspection. She approved of my shoes and my socks, re-arranged my scarf so that no part of my throat was left uncovered. She removed my cap and replaced it with a heavier specimen as well as feeling the texture of my gloves and the quality of my overcoat. She already had a more than nodding acquaintance with the texture of the garment but habit dies hard and I would have to admit that nobody has my welfare more at heart than that gracious, glorious, lifelong companion.

'Try not to indulge in liquor until tonight,' she said, 'and then we can all have a few together.' I agreed or maybe it was the accumulated wisdom of three score and ten that made me fulfil the obligation without a second thought. Outside the air was crisp. There was a frosty nip and the sky overhead was blue. What more could a man wish for at the beginning of his daily peregrinations unless it was the occasional flurry of snow to emphasise the season. No sleet thank you for the good reason that sleet can't make up its mind whether its snow, rain or good round hailstone – hailstone, blessed ambassador from the court of winter. I will now proceed with my tale and won't be waylaid again.

The streets were bright and festive with the trappings of Christmas and everywhere could be heard the joyful exchanges of the season. On a personal basis I was greeted on countless occasions and was quick to return the compliments. When I had exhausted the main streets I briefly visited the town's two squares where further seasonal exchanges were the order of the morning.

Then I took myself to the side streets and thence to the back-ways, almost always favoured by the middle-aged and the elderly because of the absence of bustle. It was here I encountered a doughty middle-aged damsel who held the centre of the back-way against all comers. She also moved at an alarming pace despite being burdened with two large bags of groceries. She had, on her flushed face, a look of intense determination. In an earlier age with a sword in her hand she would have put to flight any foe foolhardy enough to challenge her. My sixth sense, which I always keep handy, warned me that I might be better advised to forego the normal Christmas wishes and continue on my way as though she did not exist.

My sixth sense is rarely wrong but I am a man who has always cherished the belief that passers-by are there to be saluted or greeted or whatever.

'A Happy Christmas!' I ventured.

There was no verbal response but she threw me a look which suggested that she had little time for frivolities. She barged by, her sturdy steps a challenge to anyone who might dispute her right to the middle of the back-way. All the other people I saluted on that resplendent morning returned the greeting with interest.

It was around that time that I began to feel peckish so I decided upon a short-cut home. There is truly no place like home when the pangs of hunger announce their arrival so I set off with a cheerful heart to the pork chops and mashed parsnips which awaited me.

I have often thought, since that eventful morning, how we fail to take account of the possibility of disaster when we find ourselves on the crest of a wave. How beautifully Robbie Burns put it when he ploughed the mouse's nest:

> The best laid schemes of mice and men
> Gang aft a-gley
> And leave as nought but grief and pain
> For promised joy.

A flight of starlings, dipping and soaring, chirping and chatting, flew by overhead while sturdy sparrows fed on motes and grains, impervious to the passing human.

Suddenly, for a second time, I braced myself as the doughty damsel bearing the grocery bags hove into view once more. It was obvious from her demeanour that things had not been going her way all morning. Ever a believer in the power and goodness of salutation I tendered the compliments of the season again. This time she stopped and looked me up and down without reply. Then she placed her bags on the ground and looked me in the eye.

'Bad cess to you,' she spat, 'with your Happy Christmas. How could I be happy and my husband drunk in some dive and me with no way of getting home?'

I was about to say something but could think of nothing appropriate. She then sent me about my business with a four letter word followed by one of three.

For all that, the sun still shone down and the white frost faded on the roof-tops. None the worse for my encounter I stopped and bestowed the compliments of the season on a trio of people I thought I knew.

'You have some gall to salute us after what you and your crowd did to this poor girl here.'

The rebuke came from the woman probably in her late thirties, obviously the mother of the girl allegedly wronged by myself and my crowd. But who were my crowd and what had we done to the innocent who stood before me? Her husband stood idly by and made no attempt to speak and why should he with a spouse as articulate as the woman beside him. As I recall, although no word escaped his lips, he had adopted a supporting attitude.

'How did I wrong this girl?' I asked.

'The poem,' came back the prompt reply.

'What poem?' I asked.

'The poem she entered for your competition,' she answered.

'What competition?' I asked patiently.

Suddenly the words burst forth, one forcing the one before forward until a great spate of language told me that the competition had been organised by a food manufacturing company with a head office in London and that her daughter had managed to qualify for the final stages but had been deprived of her just rights by myself and my evil cronies. She went on to say that we would never have an hour's luck and that we would never die in our beds after which we would rot in hell and be damned forever without hope of redemption.

I explained that I did not belong to the organisation she had mentioned and had never, in fact, any dealings good, bad or indifferent with the food group in question at which she spewed verbal fire in all directions so that even her husband's face began to register alarm.

The victim, a shy creature on the verge of her teens, seemed as if she was going to burst into tears. I pointed out that I had once been a judge in a poetry competition sponsored by Listowel Writers' Week but had never been involved with any other.

It was as though I had slapped her face. She rounded on me once more and berated me as if I was the scum of the earth. When she had exhausted herself I extended my hands and apologised profusely for the perfidy of dishonest judges everywhere. I infused the last dregs of my drained compassion into my tone but she was having none of it. Suddenly I altered my course as it were. I remarked on the singular beauty of the morning and how it was a shame that the fine weather had not come sooner. I then veered in the direction of their Christmas dinner and enquired if they had invested in a hen or a cock turkey or maybe like myself they had opted for a goose. She replied by swinging her umbrella at me. I was, of course, totally innocent of the charge laid at my door and begged her to take note of the facts. It was only then I deduced that the creature was intoxicated. At that moment a countryman passed and asked what was wrong. I had seen him before. His face was always belligerent.

'This girl,' my tormentor pointed out, 'sent a poem to this man's competition and they sent the poem back saying it was too late for entry.'

So the charge had taken a new twist and it was possible that on this occasion she was telling the truth, except that it wasn't my competition.

'Well,' I explained, 'the rules are there and when an entry is late it is returned to the owner.'

'Scandalous isn't the word for it,' said the new arrival, the hostility rampant in his attitude.

'And suppose,' said the mother of the victimised poetess, 'that it was Shakespeare sent it would you return it? Indeed you would not for if you did you'd have no Shakespeares and you'd have no omelettes.'

At least it sounded like omelettes but of course she meant *Hamlet* but had dropped her haitch having spent a period working in London before returning to Ireland. The gentleman who had stopped to ask what was wrong had passed a disparaging remark about poetry and was now at the receiving end of the umbrella. He crumbled like a gangly puppet and rolled to safety without a whimper. My time had come too. I felt I had suffered enough but how's that Shakespeare puts it:

> When sorrows come, they come not single spies
> But in battalions.

When I arrived home I was informed that my beloved wife had accepted a lift to the funeral of a distant relative in an equally distant village. As always she had left my dinner in a covered plate on a saucepan of hot water but on this occasion there was nothing in the nature of a dinner to be seen. Apparently a handyman had called to sweep out the back-yard and he presumed that the dinner was for him and why would he presume otherwise when, on so many times in the past, he had found his dinner waiting as mine had been waiting, until he came along. According to a friend of my wife's who had called to deliver a religious magazine to which we unfailingly subscribed and unfailingly never read, the handyman had bolted my dinner in jig time and declared it to be the best so far.

I settled for a snack as I recall and, not for the first time, decided to rediscover the fine flavour of a lightly-mustarded ham sandwich. The ham was totally rotten so I decided upon a cheese sandwich but there was no cheese. At this stage I was about to fume but instead I sat down and composed myself. Slowly but surely I began to realise what a fortunate fellow I was. Here I was, unscathed after wading through a sea of troubles. I began to rejoice and when I went out into the back-yard still brightly lit by the winter sun and showing the sickle of distant Ramadan materialising in the heavens, I raised my hands aloft and thanked God for my happy lot and for allowing me to share Christmas with the less fortunate. The trials I had experienced were merely joys in disguise and the people I met were surely angels in our midst for they reminded me of my happy lot and is this not the brief of angels! For the moment farewell dear friends and a Merry Christmas and a Happy New Year to all of us.

The Resurrection

The widows of the deceased footballers blessed themselves and rose as one from the Marian shrine where they had offered an open-air Rosary for the success of the living footballers who would represent the townland of Ballybee on the following Sunday. On their coats, blouses and frocks they proudly wore the black and yellow colours of the Ballybee Gaelic football team. For the first time in twenty-four years Ballybee found themselves in the final of the junior championship.

None was more surprised than the players themselves. Rank outsiders at the beginning, they had played their hearts out in pulsating game after pulsating game until they reached the ultimate stage of the Canon Coodle Cup. Nonie Regan, mother of the team's youthful captain Shamus, prophesied from the beginning that the cup would come back to Ballybee.

'They have the youth,' she pointed out solemnly, 'and you won't beat youth at the end of the day.'

Before the first round of the championship she found few to agree with her but how different it was now! The team had grown in wisdom and experience and her son Shamus was being mentioned for the county team. It was widely believed by experienced non-partisans that the up-and-coming midfielder had the beating of his opposite number on the Ballybo fifteen, the redoubtable Badger Loran a veteran of seven finals, five of which had been annexed by Ballybo. Despite the rise and rise of the opposition they were still money on favourites to hold on to the crown.

Canon Cornelius Coodle after whom the cup was named had been a formidable footballer in his day and although extremely cautious in his footballing prognostications was inclined to favour Ballybee, 'but,' he cautioned his two curates, one from Ballybee and the other from Ballybo, 'there will be very little in it in the end and I wouldn't be at all surprised if it turned out to be a draw.'

On the morning of the game he gave one of his more memorable sermons, recalling his own footballing days and emphasising the need for sportsmanship when tempers flared and caution was likely to be thrown to the winds. He recalled sporting encounters from the past and congratulated the six other teams representing six townlands who failed to make it to the final.

'In many ways,' he explained, 'you are just as important as the finalists and with luck there might have been a different outcome in many of the games. You played like men and you behaved like men when the final whistle was blown. You shook hands with the victors and you withdrew gracefully from the scene to ready yourselves for future encounters when the day may be yours.'

The canon then addressed himself to the finalists in particular, pointing out that the children of the parish would be watching on that very afternoon and it behoved the players from both sides to set an example of sportsmanship and discipline. 'Moderate your language at all times,' he urged, 'and take into account the feelings of the referee when you feel like upbraiding him. He is only flesh and blood like all of us and he has a wife and children like many of you so be sure to take his delicate position into account before you threaten him with fist or boot. Remember that there will be songs about this great event, songs which will be sung rousingly in years to come when the combatants have passed on. What matters most is the game so see to it that you abide by the rules and in so doing you'll bring glory to your townlands and to your parish. It is my duty also to warn blackguards and thugs that the football field is for football and I shall be keeping a close eye on the goings-on at all times.'

Canon Coodle went on about excessive drinking and displays of drunkenness on the streets which scandalised young folk in particular. 'To me has fallen the honour of throwing in the ball and I hope the players from both sides will shake hands as gracefully at the close as they did at the beginning.'

Later in the day he would throw in the ball after the referee had called him on from the side-line and then he would withdraw to his cushioned chair where he would maintain a dutiful silence until the game ended.

Let us now look at the captains, firstly the Badger Loran, a forty year old midfielder, gnarled and bony and tough as wax, reputed to have broken more bones than a butcher and closed more eyes than any sleeping potion. A strong farmer unmarried and independent with a shock of grey hair which is why he was nicknamed the Badger in the first place. He entertained romantic feelings for the Widow Regan especially since her husband died but had never made his notions known for fear of rebuff. He played with distinction for the county team in his twenties but was still a force to be reckoned with at this level despite his age.

'He's no thoroughbred,' his supporters would tell anyone who cared to listen, 'but the Badger will still be in the running when the thoroughbreds are spent.'

Shamus Regan the Ballybee captain was of average height but physically he was gloriously realised and the fleetest of the thirty players who would contest the leather that day. He could go higher for the ball than any mortal in the eight townlands that made up the ancient parish. Barely gone eighteen he would need a little more weight and a little more muscle if he was to advance to county honours.

'When he's nineteen or twenty,' Canon Coodle informed his curate, 'he'll be a far tougher proposition.'

Shamus because of his blonde, curling locks was instantly recognisable wherever he went and was often a target for the scoundrels mentioned in Canon Coodle's sermon.

'They'll never nail him,' the canon wagged a finger at his assistants. 'He's too elusive, too speedy and built to ride the hardest tackle.'

'Wait till the Badger's done with him,' the curates cautioned humorously.

'He'll annihilate him,' said one hoping to draw the canon's fire.

'He'll pulverise him,' said the second hoping to do the same.

'And I'll pulverise you two,' the canon countered with a laugh, 'if you don't get out of here this very minute and start hearing Confessions.'

In truth the widow's blonde-haired son could do with an extra year but he was well compensated with speed and skill.

From an early hour the supporters began to arrive in town. Most made straight for the pubs which had early openings and extended openings for the occasion. Restaurants and sweet shops did a roaring trade and the contrasting colours were quickly sold out, the black and yellow of Ballybee and the red and white of Ballybo.

Mental Nossery the poet had been in the throes of competition for several days. 'Mental isn't his right name at all' the canon would explain to visitors but the locals like to nickname those they don't fully understand. Mental, a still gangly chap of middle age, stood on a barrel in Crutley's pub and read an appropriate verse from the epic he had started as soon as the finalists were made known.

'No talking now,' Fred Crutley ordered as he smote upon the bar counter with a large wooden mallet. Mental Nossery might be mental and he might be an odd-ball but the part of him that was a poet was sacred and must therefore be respected.

'Order now please,' Blossom O'Moone, barmaid for the day, called. Slowly an uncertain silence began to make itself felt. It was neither the time nor the place for poetry but Blossom would agree that a poet was a poet and might not be available the day after or the day after that or for indeed many a day especially this poet for he had received the annual rent for his leased farm only the day before. That was part of the agreement which both parties had signed, payment on the day or the nearest working day prior to the final of the football championship.

Fortified with three freshly-consumed whiskeys and one pint of stout the poet raised a hand and prepared himself to read from the leaflet which fluttered in his shaking hand. He first explained to the somewhat disinterested clientele that he would be omitting most of the verses from the fourth book of the epic on account of the introductory nature of the contents, 'as for instance,' he explained to his restless listeners, 'the many verses necessary to depict the arrival of the aficionados and the names by which they are recognised locally.'

'Get on with it,' a loud voice called. It came from a whiskered elder who happened to be sporting the black and yellow colours of Ballybee. He was immediately shouted down by several raucous young gentleman who wore the red and white ribbons of Ballybo.

Without further preamble Mental Nossery started. Dramatically he extended a long lean hand to encompass his listeners as it were and with the other hand held the pages closer to his eyes: 'They came in coracle, punt and raft,' he intoned

'And every make of outrageous craft
The drunk, the doting, the damned, the daft
The lewd and the low and the lofty
On mule and jennet, on horse and ass
On pony and cob through ford and pass.
Pensioner, puler, laddie and lass
And the crass and crude and crafty.'

Mental judged from the humour of the crowd that he might be best advised to move on to the names of those who would be present on the side-lines: 'Mottled McMahons and fair McEntees,' he raised his tone:

'Black McAlackys and hairy McMees,
Bald-headed Bradys and brindled O'Deas
Committed to common obstruction
In bevvies and levies and staggering skeins
Black-toothed Bradys and buck-toothed Maines
Foxy-haired Finnertys, bow-legged Kanes
Fermenting to foster destruction.

'And now the ladies' – Mental Nossery was always mindful of the opposite sex. He often boasted that they would never be neglected while he drew breath.

'What do you think of it?' Blossom O'Moone asked of Toben the schoolmaster.

'Well,' said he, 'considering that we're landlocked here and only a small river for water, the punts and rafts and coracles show how mental the poet is.'

The clientele, those who could fully hear him, were impressed but they were not entertained. Nevertheless like any poet worthy of the name he referred to the female breeds likely to be in attendance. His rendering became pacier now as he reeled off:

Delia Dan Donies and Tessie Tom Ned's
Minnie Matt Minnie's and Freda Mick Fred's
Delectable damsels for marital beds
But presently prey to confusion
Julie Jack Josie's and Josie Jack Jim's
Katie Tom Katie's and Tessie Tom Tims
Malignantly whetted by virginal whims
And curdled for want of collusion.

This verse, alas, proved too much for a hot-headed male member of the Freda Mick Fred family who denied that his breed were ever prey to confusion. He retaliated by knocking Mental from his barrel and would have throttled him had not Blossom spirited him out of doors and sent him on his way to a safer hostelry.

As match time drew near the pubs began to disgorge their crowds and soon there was a steady stream heading towards the sports' ground where the local brass band was playing. Then suddenly there was silence as the band struck up the national anthem. After the anthem a loudspeaker was placed in the now-steady hand of Mental whose true Christian name was Indigo.

'Now, now now!' the canon raised his hands aloft for silence, 'our Laureate will regale us with a verse or two.'

The canon withdrew a step leaving the stage to the poet. For his part Mental Nossery held forth with what he believed was the kernel of the poem.

'I see Mars in the sky or to be more exact in those black clouds that have gathered to the west of us. I now formally invoke the aid of the Holy Spirit and call for ten seconds silence after which, by the grace of God, I will commence to versify:

> Up above Mars waits for the bloody fare
> The lightning brightening his burnished hair
> As he madly treads on the trembling air
> And prises the heavens asunder.
> Now he raises his hands than the welkin higher
> His nostrils belching and billowing fire
> As his voice rolls over the land entire
> With its terrible tones of thunder.
>
> Harken now to the words I say
> Let the lines be drawn for the coming fray
> Let there be no quarter this glorious day
> Let each wound another nourish.
> Let the game flow fast, let the blood flow free
> Let the ball know elbow, boot and knee

Let knuckles white set the molars free
Let the warrior spirit flourish.'

The canon applauded loudly but there was to be no more for the referee's whistle had sounded and the game was on. The play flowed freely, then savagely, then wickedly, then beautifully and gracefully as Shamus Regan sent over the opening point for Bally-bee. Ballybo responded quickly when the Badger fielded high and sent a long pass to his forward-in-chief who split the posts for the equalising point. There followed for the hour similar exchanges while the crowd roared their approval. Never had they seen such a final. Never had so many passionate tempers flared and died and flared again. Never were there so many accurate points and never before in the history of the competition were dynamic goals scored, one for either side by the captains of either team. The Badger lost his head and flayed his opponents but Shamus kept his and won a free kick which was to be the final one of the game the referee warned.

The sides were level as the Ballybee captain placed the ball, sixty full yards from the Ballybo goal. A tricky wind had crept into the proceedings towards the end of the game which made free-taking extremely diffi-cult. Add to this the acute angle of the space between ball and posts. A mortifying silence descended. The day would belong to Ballybee should the ball go over the bar. Shamus bent his head and looked not at the far-off posts. He would estimate with closed eyes before he opened them to kick the ball. Over it went and the crowd went wild. Then a scuffle broke out and when Shamus tried to intervene he was felled and kicked in the head. The Badger threw his great body across the youth to save him from further kicks.

Later in the hospital the doctors concluded that Shamus was in a coma and might well remain in that suspended state for a month or a year or forever.

Blossom O'Moone lived on the side of the street in a small house which fronted seven acres of arable land. The cows which grazed her pastures were never hungry nor were they ever smitten by disease. Blossom's maxim was that cleanliness was the answer to all ills. The milch cows, five in number, provided half of her meagre income. Odd jobs such as white-washing, scrubbing and part-time barmaid-cum-cleaner at Crutley's public house provided the other half. If she was liberal with her favours, as they said, she was also choosy. Her liaisons were short-lived and those who boasted loudest about ravishing her had never even spoken to her. Those who did not boast at all and those who kept their minds to themselves would be more likely to have received her favours or so the wise men of the locality were fond of saying.

'Not so at all,' Mrs Crutley held opposing views, 'Blossom is just a hot court. If she was anything else she would not be working under this roof.'

The house and land had been willed to her by her grandfather. Blossom's mother had succumbed to the ravages of tuberculosis in an era when there was no redress for victims of the disease. Her father's identity was a mystery.

Blonde and wispily formed she was possessed of what locals were fond of calling a quaint face. Rather was it a quizzical face. She seemed to be forever in search of mystical fulfilment although precisely what kind of mystical fulfilment no one was prepared to say. If they had been more observant they would have noticed that the quizzical look was replaced with one of concern whenever she found herself looking into the bright, blue eyes of Shamus Regan, captain of the Ballybee football team. Although twelve years his senior she felt that there was more than a mild interest. The fact that he also blushed unreservedly confirmed her suspicions. She stored him in a certain secret place in her memory and vowed to resurrect him at the earliest opportunity and she knew, however far-fetched it might seem, that opportunities always presented themselves, even on the most unlikely occasions. Presently, however, it seemed highly unlikely that there would be a moonlight tryst between them.

A small but vibrant river ran by one of the tiny fields at the rear of her house. She had planned to lure him there, to a sheltered grove near a small pool and there to bathe with him and run through the moon-lit fields with him till they fell exhausted into each other's arms but this would never happen now. It seemed certain that he would never waken from the coma in which he found himself.

The night frost had descended on the fields as she walked and whispered to herself: 'This very river flows under his window in the hospital in the town and were I to strip now down to my pelt and wear just a garment like that old fur coat Mrs Crutley gave me twelve months ago this Christmas and were I to tuck it inside my corduroy trousers and were I to pull on my wellingtons what would stop me from straying along the river-bank to the hospital and then to that small room at the back which overlooks the river. Without disturbing the drip which sustains him, slip out of my things and slip in beside him. He has no hope of coming out of the coma anyway and what harm would I be doing if I held him close and kissed his lips and stroked his curls till he stirred maybe and yielded to me? Why shouldn't I do it when there's no other hope for the poor boy? I know I have it in me to waken him. I feel a great force in me and it's driving me towards him.'

Blossom was shocked by her resolve and her intensity. Later as she moved gracefully along the bank of the shining river she recalled the many times since the football final in the summer she had made the same journey but on those occasions it had been to worship from a distance and to pray for the still creature in the lone bed of the dimly-lit ward.

'She mightn't be the full shilling,' Dr Matt Coumer told his wife as they sat drinking one night after hours in Crutley's, 'but she has mystic qualities. In another age, in another place she might have been a priestess or a sorceress.' Blossom had just served them with a drink and bestowed upon them a most mystical smile, the smile that others called quaint and quizzical. Matt shook his head after he had sipped from his glass. 'There's more to Blossom than flesh and bone,' he concluded and then he dropped the subject as they were joined outside the counter by Fred Crutley and his wife.

Blossom had little difficulty negotiating the stone steps which carried her from the river-side to the window of the ward where lay her golden boy. From a safe distance she could see all that was happening in the ward. Shamus Regan's mother sat at one side of the bed and, wonder of wonders, the Badger Loran sat at the other.

Blossom liked the Badger. He was tough, uncompromising and gnarled like an ancient thorn tree but he was respectful and in Blossom's eyes that was what mattered in a man when all was said and done.

After a while Mrs O'Regan rose and withdrew a hair brush from her coat pocket. The Badger lifted the young man's head and held it gently while Mrs Regan brushed the beautiful locks of her son's damaged head.

Blossom bent her own head over her hands and pressed her cold fingers against her forehead. A feeling of unbearable sorrow seized her as her entire body began to tremble. Then came the tears and with them a series of gentle but profound lamentations that helped to ease the pain within her. She dried her eyes with her cold hands and, still trembling, drew the fur coat tightly round her bosom.

In the ward the Badger was weeping. She had often heard people say of him that he was incapable of tears, that he could not express himself when sorrow assailed him, that's if it ever assailed him they said. If only they could see him now, Blossom thought. He sat on the side of the bed and shook his great shoulders helplessly when the widow placed tender hands thereon. She helped tease the anguish out of him. She had been taken by surprise, never having seen him shed a solitary tear until that very moment. 'It's good to cry,' she whispered and allowed her hands to caress the sides of his craggy face.

As she watched, Blossom declared to herself that such a woman would bring great ease and solace to a man and to the Badger in particular for he had held on to his feelings for too long a time and they had become frosted and crusted but Blossom sensed that he would never surrender to despair again, not with Nonie Regan by his side to comfort him.

After a long, long spell she noticed how the Badger's powerful body began to compose itself once more. Blossom knew that every person who walked the earth was possessed of a sorrow that wreaked havoc on the human heart. Age often alleviated it and so did companionship but love, mostly, was the antidote although traces of it would always remain and visit the spirit, reminding the victims of long forgotten sorrows stored in the memory.

The Badger heaved a final sigh indicating that he had put his grief behind him. Then with a flourish he produced the most voluminous handkerchief Blossom had ever seen. He trumpeted several times into its deep folds and returned it to his pocket. Then he rose and steadied himself before taking the Widow Regan in his arms. As they clung tightly to each other Blossom felt the last of her sadness leave. Then the couple bent and kissed the lifeless form in the bed. The Badger would compensate in so many ways for the illness which had destroyed all forms of normal communication between mother and son.

After they left the ward Blossom stood stock still

for a while. She had learned enough about the dark to know that it could throw up anything when one least expected it. She might well be under secret surveillance from some unknown source, good or evil. Such was the way of darkness. From the distant streets of the town came the strains of Christmas carols, gentling and purifying her spirit.

I will go now to his bedside she told herself and if it is in the power of a human heart to raise the siege of silence and lifelessness that overwhelms him it shall be done and no one will ever know what befell.

In the ward he lay still, his blonde curls still shining after his mother's ministrations. Making certain that the corridor was empty she readied herself for the loving task ahead of her. He lay still while she whispered words of endearment and womanly passion into his ear. She kissed him and caressed him and she called his name in rich whispers and then a secret smile appeared on her face. It was an expression of triumph, of surpassing achievement, a jubilant rejoicing for having attained the unattainable, for defying all the odds, for restoring life to where there had been no life and no hope of life. There should have been somebody in the wings, she felt, to emerge and ask her to take a bow. She had never in her life felt so elated. She had suddenly been transformed from a general factotum to a healer and if she never did anything else in her life this was sufficient in her eyes to justify her tenure in a world that sometimes just did not care but, mercy of mercies, sometimes did care.

As she drew her fur coat round her she heard voices in the corridor; one belonged to the matron and the other was the property of the poet Mental Nossery. Mental intoned in deep euphony the words of an ancient hymn. If the truth were known the composition wasn't ancient at all. It was Mental's latest. 'It was composed,' Mental Nossery informed the matron, 'in the year eleven hundred and ninety by the court jester on the death of his sovereign, Frederick Barbarossa.'

Suitably impressed the matron led the way into the ward where her most prized patient was sitting up in bed. If the matron had entered a few seconds earlier she might have witnessed Blossom make good her escape through the ward window, a window which she closed discreetly behind her before embracing the soothing moonlight which awaited her without. She received it eagerly and watched as the matron and Mental Nossery recovered from their shock.

The resurrection of Shamus Regan was the talk of the parish for evermore. Only two people knew the truth, Blossom and Mental Nossery.

Mental had arrived at the hospital only moments after Blossom but whereas she had entered by the back entrance he had entered by the front. When he arrived at the door of the ward he heard strange sounds, sounds which he would normally associate with another place in other circumstances. In the half light of the ward he deduced that there was an extra body in the bed, most certainly, judging from the sounds emerging from her lips, a female.

Later, as Mental Nossery left the hospital grounds he was waylaid by Blossom. He told her what had happened.

'I was about to enter the ward,' he explained, 'when I heard the unmistakable sounds of wild oats being sown. There were two participants in this wonderful activity so I presumed that Shamus had awakened or been awakened from his long sleep. The great thing is that he'll be all right from now on or so the matron and the two doctors who arrived hot-foot assured everybody.'

'It's a wonderful night entirely,' Blossom exclaimed with delight. She took Mental by the hand and led him to the river-bank by which secret route they journeyed hand in hand to the abode of Blossom. First they walked her small fields under the light of an indulgent moon and then they withdrew to her cosy kitchen.

They married the following autumn and Mental Nossery no longer rented his lands. His proud wife who was an accomplished farmer in her own right saw to his verdant acres as well as her own. After some time Blossom produced a young son and not long after that Mental Nossery finished his epic. Canon Cornelius Coodle wrote the ten thousand words introduction and the poem was hailed far and wide. In that same summer Shamus Regan received his call for the county team and just before the September equinox of the same year the Badger Loran and Nonie Regan walked up the aisle together. As they left the church after the ceremony they were greeted by a jerseyed guard of honour consisting of members from the football teams of Ballybee and Ballybo.

DOTIE TUPPER'S CHRISTMAS

When Dotie Tupper retired from the fowl business at the age of eighty-four she decided to take a holiday. The first thing she did when she arrived at her home on the very day she gave up work was to immerse herself in a bath of warm water and remain there for the best part of an hour. In so doing she was merely following the habit of a life-time. There were no toilet facilities at her place of work save an antiquated WC frequented solely by Sam Toper. She avoided it as if it was an execution chamber. Whenever she felt overpowered by the offensive stenches in her workplace or felt in need of a wash she made the short trip to her modest home a few doors down the lane-way. Her boss Bustler Hearne never objected. He knew that Dotie would more than make up for any time she was likely to spend off the premises.

Bustler was a bully, a rude, crude and highly aggressive employer who made life hell for two of the three members of his staff, Sam Toper, fowl executioner, plucker-in-chief and trusser extraordinaire and Mannie Kent, dispatcher and part-time cleaner. Dotie Tupper was in charge of sales, wages and supervising. She also helped out when her staff found themselves unable to cope with the pressures of work or illness.

Her boss, Bustler, spent of most of his time in the countryside within a radius of ten miles of his business location. Before he left in the mornings in his horse-drawn crate-clamped dray and after he returned in the evening with crates of assorted fowl he made his presence felt by verbally and physically abusing his plucker-in-chief and by roundly cursing his cleaner. Never once during the long years that Dotie spent in his employ had he been known to direct a single harsh word at her. He also paid her a decent wage and why wouldn't he, his detractors would say, and she coining money for him on all fronts. Certainly it would be true to say that she had made him a wealthy man. She also made a name for him as a supplier of high-quality produce. She was courteous to customers and when part-time staff were taken on at Christmas she taught them how to truss and pluck. In an emergency Dotie could wring a chicken's neck in a flash and on occasion in a matter of minutes had been known to dispatch an entire crateful to their eternal rewards if such otherwordly consolation is granted to the souls of departed fowl.

Dotie was a deeply religious person and with the canon's housekeeper, the redoubtable Mrs Hannie Hanlon, was in charge of the floral arrangements behind the church altar, was a chorister in the parish choir and an esteemed member of the Trallock Parish Amateur Drama Group sometimes known as the Trallock Players. It could be said that Dotie was a participant in the game of life and not a mere looker-on. She gave herself unstintingly to all worthwhile causes and when she gave Bustler a months' notice on the first of May he went on his knees before her and begged her to remain. She shook her head firmly even when he offered her a substantial raise, shorter hours and longer holidays as well as bonuses, bribes and assorted perks.

'I am eighty-four,' she announced firmly, 'and I

am no longer able for the work.'

Fortunately for Dotie Bustler had contributed to a personal pension scheme on behalf of himself and his prize employee of over sixty-eight years. She had started off her poultry career with Bustler's father Toby, brought him from the verge of bankruptcy and set his son firmly on the road to prosperity.

Bustler was a hot-tempered, intemperate thug or so it was claimed by those who maintained they knew him. He was possessed, however, of one virtue. He was a generous man and when Dotie departed she did not go empty-handed. During the years as an employee she managed to present a spotlessly clean appearance to the world. Not so her fellow-employees, Mannie Kent and Sam Toper. Sam's Sunday suit was mottled with the stains of partly-erased fowl droppings and tiny traces of down and feathers while his workaday overalls had changed from light blue to off-white over the years.

Mannie also carried traces of down and other fowl specks from her place of employment on her every-day clothes. On the other hand Dotie, even while at work, presented a shining image to the public. Small and spare she had a capacity for endless work. Without fail, no matter her disposition at the time, she always had a bath after work. When showers became the mode she showered on Saturdays and Sundays. She spent her summer holidays in the nearby seaside resort of Ballybunion. She always stayed at Collins' guesthouse and went for a hot seaweed bath every day of her richly deserved fortnight.

'Regular bathing,' she once told her life-long

friend Mickey Mokely, 'is the only antidote for the job I'm in.'

For years before she retired she was invited by her dear friend Hannie Hanlon, Canon Coodle's house-keeper, to spend the Christmas holiday at the presby-tery. Hannie had free rein at the parochial house but nevertheless thought it prudent to consult with the canon beforehand.

'She's as near to an angel,' the canon had noted at the time, 'as anyone we're likely to encounter in this world.'

So it was that in her eighty-fourth year she was still a welcome guest at the presbytery for the Christ-mas period except that this time she would stay for the extended sojourn of the Twelve Days. In the town she was a popular figure. Young and old called her by her first name, Dotie. 'Ah she's a dotie girl to be sure,' Fr Sinnott the senior curate announced when he fre-quently picked her up, placed her under his arm and laid her on the bottom step of the stairs after doing the rounds of the presbytery with her. Her bright presence brought joy and goodness wherever she went and yet deep down she carried a great hurt. Hannie knew about the hurt and the absent-minded canon had his suspicions. Absent-minded the canon might be about inanimate things but when he cared for people he was ever ready to listen to their woes and extend the hand of compassion where it was needed.

'There is a message clearly written on Canon Coodle's face,' Fr Sinnott once informed his bishop, 'and what it says is this – "I am here for you my friend no matter how high up or low down you are. I don't care what you have done. I am always here for you".'

'I've seen it,' said the bishop, 'and I thank God that it's there for all of us.'

The pair were returning from the all-Ireland Gaelic Football Final in Dublin chauffeured by a junior curate who neither drank nor smoked. He had been specially chosen by his parish priest, an astute gentleman who had seen both the bishop and Fr Sinnott play football and remarked more than once that he was truly grateful to his maker that he had never crossed the path of either on the playing field.

Among his other virtues, the junior curate in question was also possessed of sealed lips and subscribed to the ancient Chinese adage that a shut mouth caught no flies. If his Lordship and Fr Sinnott had a failing it was merely a shared love of an occasional indulgence in a few pints of stout, well, a good few pints of stout but not on a regular basis. Hence the necessity for an abstemious and close-mouthed driver.

On the Christmas of her eighty-fourth year Dotie arrived at the presbytery as usual. She was glad to be leaving her home for a while although a bright and cosy home it was and a home which she hoped to share with her dear friend Hannie should Canon Coodle pass on as indeed he must some day but as Hannie would say 'let us pray that it's a far-off day and that I will be there to look after him until such time as that day comes'. At the canon's insistence Dotie always had her meals in the parochial dining-room.

On the Christmas Eve of that eighty-fourth Christmas Dotie was, according to Hannie, down in herself.

'Well then,' said Canon Coodle, 'we must do all in our powers to cheer her up.'

The topic of conversation at the tea-time table had been the return of the presbytery cat, a battle-scarred chap who had, from the looks of him when he returned, surely forfeited his penultimate life of the nine lives granted to all cats. Fond of a scrap and fiercely possessive of his many female friends it was inevitable that he would meet physically more accomplished Toms during his ramblings on moon-lit roof-tops under starry skies when only cats are abroad. He slunk into the dining-room and rubbed his racked body against the canon's left shoe.

'Ah my friend,' said Canon Cornelius with a grim smile, 'what a mighty confession you could make at this moment.'

It was the first genuine laugh that Dotie had enjoyed in several weeks. Her woes had really begun when it began to dawn on her that she would never see her father again, not in this world anyway. Always, up until her eighty-fourth birthday she cherished the faint hope that he would one day return. She remembered him only vaguely. She had been six years of age when he disappeared a month after her mother's death. There were ugly whispers abroad that while he was of unsound mind after his bereavement he might well have eased himself into the flooded river in the belief that he might be united with the woman who had been the love of his life. Then there were rumours that he had been seen in places as far apart as Glasgow and Chicago. Each night, from the age of six onwards Dotie prayed for his safe return. At first she could not believe that he had walked out on her. She had missed her mother terribly at the time but with the passage of the years it was for her father she longed. She had seen other girls out walking with their fathers. She had bitten her lip in anguish when she saw small girls being lifted into the air by the one man they loved above all others in the world. She had cried herself to sleep on countless nights. Her aunt who had come to look after her and who slept in the adjoining room would silently slip into the bed beside her and do her best to console her. There were times when she thought she saw her father but it was always from a distance so she could not be certain.

'I don't have any doubt,' the district inspector of the RIC had made clear at the time. 'His behaviour was strange to say the least for days before his disappearance. He was seen by the river-side at a point where once in, it would be impossible to change one's mind. He knew what he wanted to do and he did it. That is my conclusion and it is the conclusion of all the other investigators involved.'

Dotie steadfastly refused to believe that her father was not coming home and now at eighty-four she knew in her heart that she would not see him again.

'One would imagine,' she told herself, 'that I would be over it by now but I will never be over it,' she cried out in the confines of her kitchen. The worst was that she could not remember sitting on his lap while he sang.

'I remember the pair of you well,' her aunt recalled not realising how deeply wounded Dotie became at mention of her father. 'He used to sit on the old rocking chair on the porch and you would climb aboard his lap. He had a light tenor voice but he never sang after your mother died. He never meant to leave you. He wasn't himself the Lord be good to him and how could he after his terrible loss? We must pray for him. We must always pray for him.'

All through the years from the age of six to eighty-four she simply could not reconcile herself with his disappearance. In the early years she convinced herself that he was a victim of amnesia. She invented other excuses when the long decades went by and he failed to show up. At length she resigned herself to the sad fact that he was gone forever.

'He would be a hundred and twelve years of age next Saturday week.' She forced a laugh as she disclosed the information to Hannie Hanlon. Hannie had remained silent not knowing what to say.

'I was reading lately in one of the Sunday papers,' Dotie continued, 'that the oldest man in the world was one hundred and eleven years of age. I was going to write to the editor and tell him that if my father was alive he would be the oldest man in the world and then I thought how foolish I would look if he decided to publish the letter.'

Still not knowing how to respond Hannie waited for her friend to continue. Dotie's voice was no longer steady as she spoke. 'Imagine it took me all those years before I finally realised he was well and truly dead and not coming home anymore. I always cherished the hope that he might somehow make his way back to me but at a hundred and twelve it would be out of the question. I still have his photographs, one in particular, the one taken before he shaved off his moustache. My but he was handsome and so tall. I don't know where they got me because my mother was a tall woman too. If I could be sure I would see him again, see the two of them again somewhere someplace I would die happy.'

Hannie placed a hand around her friend's shoulder but she couldn't find the proper words of consolation so she steered her out of the room and into the hall-way.

'I don't remember sitting on my father's lap while he sang to me and that's the hardest part,' Dotie was weeping now. 'I know for a fact that my aunt saw me sitting with him but I have no recollection of it.'

Dotie had just reached the age of sixteen when her aunt died, a victim of tuberculosis, the same disease that accounted for her mother. Relatives and friends decided that it would be best for Dotie if she emigrated to the United States where her only surviving aunt was settled but when Toby Hearne offered her a job Dotie had no hesitation in accepting. Neighbours and friends feared for her well-being at the hands of such a man but Dotie had no qualms. She was possessed of that rare quality which always brought out the best in people and like so many others Toby quickly fell under her spell. When he would rant and rave at others Dotie would look on in amusement knowing that his rage would expend itself in a few short minutes. Over the years she managed to temper his and Bustler's outbursts and around the time she decided it was time to retire Bustler's nature had assumed a mellow side which eventually won out over his dark side. She went so far as to suggest to him that he retire. The business was but a shadow of what it used to be but Bustler had made his money particularly during the period of the Second World War and he had invested it wisely always acting on Dotie's advice.

Rather than sell the business he closed it on his ninetieth birthday and retired to a local old folks home where he spent the remainder of his days. He regularly visited the premises where he spent his entire life and when he died his last will and testament revealed that the sole beneficiary from his estate was none other than Dotie.

When Bustler withdrew from his business the same notion of retiring occurred to Canon Cornelius Coodle – but he quickly dismissed the thought when it dawned on him that he would be contributing to the unprecedented scarcity of priests in the diocese. He told himself that he would be the last man to leave down the side.

'I'll die in my harness,' he told the wrinkled face which confronted him in the mirror of his bedroom.

After late Mass that night he withdrew to the sitting-room with Fr Sinnott. The canon raised his brimming glass of port and wished his senior curate the compliments of the season. Fr Sinnott responded and sipped from his tumbler of Jameson.

'Ah!' he exclaimed as Dotie and Hannie entered, 'the ladies are with us.'

Both priests rose and toasted the fresh arrivals who returned the seasonal compliments by touching the extended glasses of the clergymen with the delicate sherry glasses shapely and brimming. As they settled into their chairs the canon began to reminisce about past events in his life as was his wont on Christmas Eve. He noted, for all his pre-occupation with other days, that all was not well with Dotie. It was Hannie who explained that Dotie was facing up to the fact that she would not see her father again and worse still that she could not remember sitting on his lap when she was a little girl.

'What age would he be now if he was alive?' Fr Sinnott asked with no little amazement.

'One hundred and twelve,' Dotie replied without a moment's hesitation as the tears flowed down her face.

Fr Sinnott extended his hands in her direction after placing his glass on the floor beneath his chair. Dotie handed her glass to her friend Hannie and a new hope surged within her. The senior curate's powerful hands were still extended towards her, the same hands that had subdued countless ambitious full forwards and the same hands that once held aloft the county championship Gaelic football trophy which was his inalienable right as captain. In his lap Dotie looked up into his face and in a little girl's voice asked the question which had been troubling her so much in recent times.

'Will I see my dad again?' she asked.

'Of course you will,' Fr Sinnott assured her

'But will he know me?'

'Will he what!' Fr Sinnott shouted, 'you'll be sore for six months woman for the squeezing he'll give you.'

A radiant smile adorned the tear-stained face of Dotie.

'And my mother!' she directed the question at Canon Coodle.

'Of course, of course,' Canon Coodle assured her, 'she'll be there at the gates of heaven by your father's side and the three of you will enter heaven together.'

Dotie's eyes were closed in bliss. Fr Sinnott rose with his charge cradled in his arms. He walked round the room a few times humming softly and paused in front of his canon's armchair. 'You take her for a while,' he said, 'and I'll fill another drink.'

Canon Coodle placed her carefully on his lap and gently kissed her on the forehead. A succession of reassuring and audible murmurs escaped him before he cleared his throat and crooned a lullaby from the Gaelic. It had been his grandmother's song when he was a small boy.

A Christmas Gander

There's many a regal gander no more than a skeleton in his pelt. How often did goose buyers find it out in the past to their cost? It's different these days when geese and ganders arrive on the Christmas market deprived of their downy raiments, their feathers and their wings. One can easily tell the elderly from the prime and if they are mass-produced itself the buyer will not be duped and if they lack the true flavour of pasture-land geese at least the flesh can be eaten if boiled or roasted properly.

Country people used to believe in those distant days that the shore gander was the best proposition of all because of his delightful flavour. His diet, apart from grass and his daily saucer of yellow meal, consisted mainly of molluscs, cuttle fish, slokawn or sloke and lavenworth. Is it any wonder there was such demand for shore ganders! It was also believed that the soup from boiled ganders of the seashore species was a priceless antidote for scrofulous diseases as well as being a proven booster for middle-aged and elderly males whose romantic input into their marital obligations was declining. After a few plates of shore gander soup they generally excelled themselves.

Every time there is a Christmas in the offing my thoughts unfailingly turn to geese. Some people prefer turkeys while more have a preference for ducks and drakes and cockerels but it's the goose for me, the roast stuffed goose preceded by giblet soup. My mouth waters as I summon up remembrance of bygone ganders.

Just before this very Christmas I engaged two from a country cousin, a woman of impeccable credentials in the matter of geese and ganders. In dark moments and troublesome times I think of these very geese, browned and roasted and my heart soars like an uprising lark.

If you have ever been taken down in the purchase of a goose that is to say if you buy an old goose thinking it to be a young goose you will never again engage geese hastily nor will you buy at random from any Tom, Dick or Harry. To be quite candid I would put the same amount of preparation and planning into the purchase of a goose as I would into the robbing of a bank. Too many times in the past I was taken down by otherwise honest people. In the countryside it was never considered a dishonest act to dispose of elderly or decrepit geese to gullible townies. Old geese must be sold and who better to sell them to than townies. Few townies knew the identities or dwelling-places of goose producers so the producer is generally safe from retaliation. In addition nearly all people who sold geese looked alike. That is to say they were possessed of kind, honest faces especially these who foisted off ancient birds on the unwary and unsuspecting.

In my boyhood Christmases you would always find the rogue producers in that corner of the market where the donkey and pony transports were thickest and the smiling saleswomen would always call you sir, even if you were the biggest rogue in the world. Luckily for me I have now, near the end of my days, accrued some experience in the engaging and purchase of geese.

At the tender age of twelve I was sent to the market-place in my native town having been commissioned to invest in a prime goose for an elderly neighbour who should have known better. She was too old to go herself and even at the age of eighty she still had a good deal of faith in humanity. It was foolishly presumed at the time that I was street-wise. The word had yet to make its way into our everyday vocabulary. Crafty was the word used in those days but unfortunately I was not crafty enough to match the wily and seasoned dealers anxious to dispose of ancient geese.

Earlier that morning I received a short instruction in the ways of geese. Old geese, for instance, like their human counterparts were somewhat listless. Their eyes too were lack-lustre. Their beaks were worn down and were of a darker hue than those of young geese. The laipeens (feet) were wrinkled and coarse. These were some of the better-known defects to be found in geese and ganders of advanced years. This information was conveyed to me by the husband of the good lady who liked a goose for Christmas. He reminded me too that young ganders were aggressive, raucous chaps who liked to flap their wings and intimidate people going about their lawful business. Armed with this vast array of knowledge and clutching two florins in my trousers' pocket I entered the market. In those days trousers generally accommodated only one pocket and the lining was never truly trustworthy. Holes infiltrated and coins disappeared. Heartbreak followed and hunger too and all sorts of deprivation especially if the sum was substantial.

Great was the clamour of geese and turkeys in the market-place not to mention ducks, drakes, hens and chickens. For once there were more women than men. It was held by even the most hostile of males in those days that turkey money was female money and should be used by females as they saw fit but the truth was that most of the money was spent on special commodities which would sweeten and brighten Christmas in the home.

As I moved here and there I was obliged to pick my steps. Ass and pony-rails cluttered the scene. Everywhere bargains were being struck and satisfied clients were departing with cross-winged braces of prime fowl. So numerous were the geese on every side that I hardly knew where to begin. I was almost overcome by the great and colourful array of transports and country folk, by the quick-fire exchanges of notes and silver, by the back-slapping and hand-slapping as bargains were struck and by the many minor altercations which eventually came to nought. It was almost too much for me and I fervently wished that I hadn't been saddled with so much responsibility.

'Ah!' said a friendly voice behind me. 'It's yourself is it' – with that he thrust out his hand and almost shook it free from my elbow joint with the shaking he gave it. I had never seen him before in my life but the more I examined his friendly face the more I began to recognise certain familiar traits. I didn't know it then but what I recognised were constituents common to the universal face of roguery. It was the friendliness of his smile that disarmed me and exposed my defence.

'I know what brought you,' he said, 'you're looking for a turkey for your mother.'

'No,' I told him, 'I'm looking for a goose for oul' Maggie Sullivan.'

'If you are,' said he, 'you'd better draw away from here,' and he winked in the most conspiratorial way you ever saw. I followed him past rails of gobbling turkeys, quacking ducks and hissing ganders.

'Half of these,' my new-found friend announced, indicating the owners of the fowl all around us, 'would nick the eye out of your head or,' said he in a loud whisper into my ear, 'if you was innocent enough to stick out your tongue that's the very last you'd see of it.'

He stopped at a corner of the market where an elderly, shawled woman with a wrinkled face was attending to an ass-rail of geese. She had, I recall to this very day, the kindest and homeliest face one could wish to see. Her voice was soft and sweet and as near to Gaelic in sound and rhythm as English could be. More to the point she had geese for sale.

'Stall-fed, every one of 'em,' she boasted, 'and not one of 'em that isn't a Michaelmas goose for sure.'

I had heard of Michaelmas geese or Green geese before this. What the term meant was that they had matured and would have been ready to eat at Michaelmas which falls on 29 September. However for extra substance and flavour they would have been confined to stalls or small out-houses till it was time for the Christmas market. The confinement meant that they would be unable to move about as much as geese normally do in the grazing area out of doors. Consequently the thighs would be less muscular and far more edible when cooked and also that the breast would be possessed of more meat and would be more succulent.

My newly-acquired friend was now standing in the rail conducting a closer inspection of its occupants. They hissed and honked as he lifted them one by one to make sure that there was no impostor among them. When he had concluded his examination he explained my predicament, how my purchasing power was restricted to four shillings and how I had been warned about dishonest vendors who would think nothing of fobbing off an elderly goose on an innocent townie.

'Oh may the good God succour us all,' said the old woman, 'and may God in his mercy preserve us, the young and the old and the innocent, from them that would wrong law-abiding people. May the flames of hell singe their yalla hides and may St Peter turn 'em back at the gates of heaven and keep them waiting for a hundred years.' She made the sign of the cross with her Rosary beads and would have continued with her excoriation had not my friend raised his hand to his lips to remind her that the evening light would soon be fading and there was a long road home.

'This man is a townie,' he explained, 'and you may be sure he has other business that needs looking after.'

'What about this one?' my friend was asking.

'No, no, no,' she was quick to reply, 'that oul' codger only came along as a companion so's the others wouldn't be too nervous on the journey. There's a sweet young gander over in the corner,' she went on, 'in the peak of condition and only out of the stall this morning.'

'Is this the lad?' my friend asked as he lifted aloft a large, hissing specimen for my approval.

'Oh the weight of him!' he cried, 'and the tenderness of him! How much are you asking for him?'

'Oh he can't be sold at all,' said the old woman, 'he's engaged by the superintendent of the civic guards.'

'Tell us what you're asking for him anyway?'

'I'm asking four shillings,' she replied reluctantly, 'but 'twould want to be handed over straightaway in case the superintendent comes along and demands what's rightfully his.'

'Sealed!' My friend extended a grimy hand for my two florins and when they had been transferred to his I found myself with the gander in my hands. My friend hurried me out of the market by a circuitous route lest, as he put it himself, I wind up in the dungeon. All the time he kept his eyes open for the presence of the superintendent and his minions.

'We'll do 'em yet!' he kept shouting, 'we'll do 'em yet!' and so we did for in a very few minutes I found myself at Maggie Sullivan's door clutching my prize.

'May God comfort us this night,' she cried out when she beheld the gander. She stood back from the pair of us to have a better look at my purchase.

'He's one age with myself,' she wept, 'if he isn't older and look at the beak worn away by him.' She called her husband and between them they set up a frightening lamentation. There was nothing for it but to return to the market, recover our two florins and invest in a younger specimen. In the market I led Maggie and her husband to the corner where the old woman had her rail but there was no sign of her. We searched the three other corners but she was nowhere to be seen. The bother was that all the old women we saw wore shawls and all had wrinkled, innocent, homely faces and you'd never believe from looking at them that any single one of them was capable of fobbing off an elderly gander on an innocent townie.

THE HERMIT OF SCARTNABROCK

Dr Matt Coumer could hardly believe his ears. The man who stood before him, as far as he knew, was the sanest and soberest in the parish. Matt had known him for most of his life. Gerry Severs lived in a small cottage by the river. He lived alone since his wife Pegeen had slipped away on him. That was the way Gerry, with his quaint turn of speech, put it when ever he was asked how his wife died. 'She slipped away on me', he would answer mournfully and then he would move hastily on lest further elaboration be required.

Matt had risen to his feet the moment Gerry entered his surgery.

'Well Gerry?' Matt asked as he proffered a hand to the young man. Not that much younger he thought, seven years, no more and no less, twenty-five years since he taught him how to cast a line and what a pupil he had been! He could land a fly in Matt's extended cap as they fished either side of the river.

'Sit down and I'll take your blood pressure.'

When Gerry failed to respond to the offer Matt countered by assuring him that there wouldn't be any charge.

'It's not blood pressure that's troubling me,' Gerry vacantly studied an anatomy chart on the wall opposite and searched for the opening words which would eventually disclose his unusual dilemma. Should he begin by telling his friend that his late, lamented wife Pegeen had been the scourge of his life from the day he had married her, that she had reviled him, spat on him, even beaten him, yes beaten him and savagely at that and that he had never reacted physically, never once. He had accepted every taunt and every jibe with resignation in the hope that she would change back into the gentle girl she had been before they married.

'I know all about Pegeen if that is what's troubling you or,' Matt paused, 'at least enough about her to know that you have suffered more than your share in your marriage.'

Gerry without turning, felt for the chair he knew to be somewhere behind him. Locating it he gratefully sat and waited for the sudden giddiness, which had visited him after Matt's revelation, to disappear.

Matt sat behind his desk and waited until some of Gerry's composure returned. After a decent interval he informed his friend how some of Gerry's neighbours who chanced to be patients of his, had asked him to intervene.

'She's a street angel and a house devil' one of Gerry's elderly neighbours had been the first to mention Pegeen's vicious behaviour. Others would follow before Matt decided to move. On that afternoon several years before as he and Gerry were fishing Matt asked him if all was well in his marriage.

'Couldn't be better,' Gerry had answered breezily.

'I'm told,' Matt would not be deterred, 'that there are serious rows.'

'A marriage without a row is like an egg without salt.'

It was the light-hearted way his friend answered that eased Matt's worries and, of course, there was the fact that neighbours exaggerated especially when they had nothing better to do.

Then one March morning earlier that year when the river was in flood, Pegeen stood barefoot on a parapet and threw herself into the swirling waters below.

'Christmas was her worst time,' Gerry spoke matter-of-factly. 'There was never a Christmas dinner but there was no scarcity of abuse. She heaped it on all through the twelve days and I took it.'

The disclosure was followed by a long silence.

'How long is she dead now?' Matt wondered if it was the right question.

'Nine months and three days,' came the forthright answer, 'and I'll tell you this Matt. I've never had such peace or at least I never had such peace until last night.'

'What happened last night?' Matt asked anxiously.

'I saw her,' came the prompt reply.

'You saw Pegeen?' Matt prompted.

'That's right,' from Gerry.

'Tell me about it.' Matt studied his friend's face for signs of instability, anything that would tell him about his mental state, studied the averted eyes for tell-tale indications of derangement and his hands for tell-tale jerks or contractions. There was nothing whatsoever to suggest that Gerry was anything other than the same, solid citizen he had always been.

'It was about half-twelve,' Gerry recalled, 'I could not sleep so I took a stroll down by the river. On my way back I felt a cold shiver all over my body. I often heard about cold shivers but I didn't believe about them until last night. A cold shiver is a nasty visitor but it's not as bad as an unnatural tremor because that's exactly what I felt shaking hands with me next.'

'An unnatural tremor you say?' Matt savoured the expression.

'Exactly,' Gerry went on, 'and on top of that I felt as if somebody had tugged at my coat but when I turned around to have a look there was nobody there or at least nobody near enough to have touched my coat. The nearest person to me at the time was a female standing under a lamp post. My heart missed a beat Matt because she was dressed exactly like Pegeen.'

'How far away was she exactly?' Matt asked.

'Forty yards to be exact,' Gerry answered without a moment's hesitation, 'and I ought to know because I played centre forward long enough to know the distance. It was then I started to shake all over. I was like a cob-web in a breeze and when I lifted my left leg to get out of there fast it wouldn't move and neither would my right leg. I was stuck there. Then a black cat came slinking out of the shadows and he passed by where the woman stood or ghost or demon or what ever because I didn't know for sure who it was at that stage. As the cat drew near the power returned to my legs but by then a courting couple had entered the square and a car also drew up close by so I felt the terror quenching itself inside of me. I said to myself I'll have a look at this woman because I'm Gerry Severs and if you ask anybody in this town what sort of bloke I am they'll tell you I'm as sound as bell metal and that I don't spin yarns. I made my way towards the dame under the pole but when I drew near to her she turned her head away. I couldn't make out her features but then the lights of the car shone full on her face and the next thing you know I was staring into her two weepers. It was Pegeen. One minute it wasn't her face and the next minute it was and when her features were exposed by the car lights there was no doubt in my mind. The blood drained out of my body and the whole square seemed to start going round in a circle. I found my balance deserting me and the sight seemed to leave my eyes. Then I began to stagger and then I fell out on my face and eyes. Look, there's a bump on my forehead and there's a cut on my poll.'

When Gerry came round he was sitting in a chair in the kitchen of a neighbour. The courting couple had seen him lying on the ground and had seen the woman walk away and had partially revived him, enough to be able to drag him to the nearest cottage in the lane-way which led from the square to the river.

Matt leaned back in his chair and closed his eyes in concentration as Gerry proceeded with his tale. Satisfied that there was no mental problem and that Gerry had been the victim of some minor hallucination which might well have been induced by the flashing car lights, he prescribed some sedatives and told him he would expect him to call around the same time on the morrow 'and by the way,' Matt went on, 'I will expect you to join my wife Maggie and myself for Christmas dinner, that's if you're free on the occasion.'

'Oh I'll manage to fit you in,' Gerry laughed, grateful of the offer because he always felt at ease in the presence of Maggie Coumer and Matt was a trusted friend of long standing. That night Matt told the whole story to Maggie.

Normally he would never disclose the contents of any exchanges whatsoever between his patients and himself but Maggie was herself a professional having qualified as a nurse many years before. 'There's no doubt but that Gerry saw a girl but there's also no doubt she could not have been his wife because if you remember it was I who laid her out when her body was recovered and it was I who helped coffin her and she was as dead as mutton you can take it from me. I'll make a few enquiries tomorrow and I'll get to the bottom of this as sure as my name is Maggie Coumer.'

That night Gerry slept soundly thanks to the sleeping capsules which his friend had given him. In the Coumer household the good doctor and his partner whispered into the morning, careful not to awaken their three young children in rooms nearby.

'I remember years ago,' Maggie recalled, 'to have been sitting in the commercial room of the Manklefort Hotel in Dublin with my brother Thady and his girlfriend. The lights were low at the time and we could barely make out each other's faces. The lights had been dimmed on the instructions of the night porter who warned us to keep our voices down because members of the garda síochána were on the prowl for illegal patrons. Shortly after he left, a passing car threw its lights through a gap in the window curtains. A shaft of this light fell on my brother's face and suddenly his features were transformed into those of my father who had died the year before. If I didn't know better I might have imagined that he had returned briefly from the dead to be with us. Then the lights were gone and the image disappeared. I remember I had never been so lonely after that brief glimpse of his face.'

'Well you're not lonely now,' Matt gently placed his arms round her and drew her close.

On the following evening after Maggie had questioned all her sources she placed her findings before her husband. He neither hummed nor hawed until she had put the facts before him. It was her wont to persevere with all her narratives without pause and instead of being bored or disinterested as some might be, Matt found himself well informed at the end of the proceedings and entertained as well.

Maggie never lingered over her revelations no matter how interesting or how salacious they might seem. Matt would settle himself at the outset and on this occasion he was well pleased for she was a woman who never lied. Of course he would have to admit that he found a certain unique musicality in her voice that he found in no other. There was also a deep warmth and never, that he could recall, had there been the least stridency or harshness. It had occurred to him on a number of occasions that it might be his affection for her that made him feel so enraptured. Still he remained convinced that an independent adjudicator would give her full marks if there was a competition for housewives' tales.

She had, apparently, discovered the identity of the mysterious woman whose face in the car light, had brought about Gerry's fainting spell. The woman was a first cousin of Gerry's late wife Pegeen and had returned home to her native parish a few short days before in the hope of meeting the man for whom she had pined since the day her cousin had married him. She had not come home for the funeral as she felt that it might have been a intrusion on her part and besides there was the protocol involved. If Gerry's affections were to be successfully transferred from his late wife to that wife's cousin then a period of at least six months should be allowed to pass. Consequently she had postponed her return until she could bear her burden no longer. She had been mortified when Gerry had collapsed after her face had been revealed to him. She had hoped that he would stop and chat or even take her in his arms but that had been a wild dream or so she admitted.

'What I propose to do,' Maggie confided to her husband, 'is invite her here for Christmas dinner and allow herself and Gerry to renew their relationship. I know, I know what you're going to say. You're going to say that it wasn't much of a relationship to begin with but my answer to that is that you cannot quench a love that burns as brightly as Noreen Meeke's and, on the other hand, Gerry will die from loneliness if he doesn't find a partner soon.'

Maggie folded her arms as she waited for her husband's appraisal. It must be said here, however, that there were many in the town who regarded Maggie as a consummate busy-body and a fully-fledged meddler. There were others, and this body included her husband, who saw her as an incurable romantic and an amateur matchmaker whose only aim was to bring lonely people together in holy wedlock. By way of arbitration Matt took his wife on his lap and kissed her gently as he complimented her on a fine afternoon's work 'for,' said Matt, 'you have accomplished two important things. You have solved a mystery which might well hang over us for many a year and you have sown the seeds of love. What more could you do on behalf of the ignorant and the lonely, on behalf of all the unfulfilled in love and knowledge? How blessed I am to have for a wife such a wonderful creature.'

Maggie beamed and blushed although she was well aware that her husband often used flowery language when he paid homage to her.

Christmas dinner at Coumer's was a rare success. Noreen Meeke was an instant success with the children and Gerry, always a favourite, added to an afternoon of unpremeditated joy. By the time the Christmas and New Year festivities ended the relationship between Gerry and Noreen was on a firm footing.

Although both were people who might be fairly described as reserved they were soon linking arms in the streets and boreens of the parish and by the time the first salmon started to run before the beginning of the fishing season there was talk of a Christmas marriage. The good doctor and his friend Gerry were unusually successful, landing a ten and twelve pound salmon respectively with two and a half inch blue minnows. The water was right for the colour and the size of bait and on the second day of legal fishing Gerry landed a second fish with the same lure. This salmon was presented to the parish priest Canon Coodle, himself a retired fisherman but now too elderly for the vicissitudes of flood-waters and gravelly streams. Long tradition obliged the first angler who bagged his second salmon of the season to present it to the parish priest. In cases where the angler might be in need the canon always paid the going rate but Gerry would not countenance financial reward.

'Tell the canon to say a prayer for me,' he informed Mrs Hanlon after she had accepted the fresh fish on her master's behalf.

'I'll do that Gerry,' she had promised, 'and I'll say one myself as well.'

The spring and summer went by and in the middle of September Gerry found himself gainful employment in Folan's timber-yard. Shortly afterwards he became engaged to Noreen Meeke and a fortnight before Christmas, to the day, the pair were married free gratis and for nothing by the legendary Canon Coodle himself.

'Don't forget in my obituary,' he wagged a cautionary finger at his friend Matt Coumer, 'to tell them about the eighteen-pounder I landed in Shanowen the very day after I was made canon of this parish.'

Matt promised the outstanding catch would be resurrected for the occasion but added the rider that should roles be reversed the nineteen-pounder he bagged at the Black Stick on his second day out must not be excluded. It was not the first time it occurred to the canon that anglers were inordinately proud of their catches and why wouldn't they be he thought defensively to himself when the average weight of a spring fish was roughly eight pounds.

As Christmas drew near the love and compassion, often buried out of sight in men's hearts, began to flow so that by the time Christmas Eve came round there was an unmistakable air of good-will and generosity all over the parish. The dour became cordial, the gripers grew cheerful, the grim grew gracious and so forth and so on until it seemed that a Christmas of untold joy was at hand. Every household radiated happiness, except one.

It had come to pass that Noreen Meeke the blushing bride of Gerry had ceased to blush, the laughter to which she had been addicted before she married vanished from her lips after marriage. In short Noreen was anything but meek and poor Gerry who was surely entitled to his fair share of marital bliss became once more a martyr to the matrimonial state. She had begun to natter early one morning as he dressed for work. The morning was dark and gloomy enough as it was without the addition of human woe to drag it down further. Gerry said nothing. He went to the side of the bed and he kissed his babbling bride to silence. Afterwards he went straight out the door to his place of work at Folan's timber-yard. He prayed that by the time he returned for his lunch she would be her old self once more but it was not to be.

There was no lunch but down from the room came a powerful verbal barrage which made Gerry believe for a moment that his late wife had been reincarnated. Trembling he opened the bedroom door and was gratified to see that it was his new wife who occupied the bed from which she was still holding forth. All the abuse wasn't directed at Gerry although it would be true to say that the greater portion of it was. She excluded none of his friends or neighbours reserving the choicer profanities for Matt and Maggie Coumer but most heinously of all she announced in a powerful voice that the flames of hell were not hot enough for Canon Coodle, his housekeeper and the two curates, a quartet, incidentally on whom until this time nobody had laid a hard word.

Vainly Gerry tried to calm her. He spoke with the utmost tenderness and reassured her of his undying love. He spoke of the wonderful Christmas they would have and of the happy times after that. He endeavoured to calm, cajole and canoodle her but all his physical efforts were rejected and all his blandishments fell on deaf ears. He spent his entire lunch break with her. That evening Matt paid her a visit and prescribed some medication.

At ten o'clock that night, without a word to anyone, Gerry betook himself to an ancient water-keeper's lodge above the river bank. It was situated about two miles outside the town and was hidden from every approach by dense natural growth. He made several journeys during the course of the night and early morning until he had accumulated sufficient clothing and utensils to meet his needs. He prepared a fire from some timber and tinder he had brought with him. He slept until noon and when he had breakfasted he spent the remaining day-light hours walking along the river bank. He had brought his rods and lines and lures with him on his final journey to the lodge. He would spend the weeks ahead preparing his fishing gear.

In the course of time Noreen recovered fully but she never mentioned her husband's name or responded to queries about his welfare. If one was to judge by appearances one would have to conclude that no happier soul existed in the parish. She was well pleased with her deserted wife's allowance and declared it to be more than adequate.

Gerry, for his part, collected his dole money by arrangement from a small shop where he would purchase all his wants for the week. The shop stood near a cross-roads about a mile from where he resided but it might as well have been a hundred for the terrain was rough and dangerous and a resort of badgers whose rooting and grunting could be heard all night. Compared to the verbal broadsides of Noreen Meeke the sounds of the wilderness were music to Gerry's ears. Any salmon he bagged was taken to the cross-roads shop which acted as an agency for a Waterford city fish buyer. Gerry ignored the other anglers who fished the waters contiguous to his domain. When saluted he grunted an acknowledgement and no more. On a few occasions from the undergrowth he spotted Matt Coumer circling the lodge but he never emerged. He blamed Matt's wife for landing him in a second disastrous marriage and wanted no more to do with her. He allowed his beard to grow and grow it did down to his naval, grimy, grey and gruesome. He became known as the Hermit of Scartnabrock.

After ten years in the wilderness he eventually fell foul of the wet and the damp and brought pneumonia upon himself. When he failed to appear for several days his friends Matt Coumer and Sergeant Ruttle went in search of him. He lay gasping his last breath on a damp bed when they found him. He managed a smile when he recognised them. It was a smile that touched Matt to the very quick of his being.

The funeral was poorly attended save for the salmon and trout anglers who fished the river from source to mouth year in, year out. They carried the coffin on their shoulders from the church to the grave-yard where Canon Coodle spoke of the kindness Gerry had shown in his healthier days to younger anglers and to strangers who were not well versed in the ways of the river. The canon spoke of Gerry's attachment to all rivers great and small and explained the influence the river had on himself especially when the dead man and he fished together in the past. He spoke about the tributaries which brought their own special flavour to the river. He spoke of the different tunes the river sang depending on the highs and lows of the ever-flowing waters. He explained how the river never sang the same song twice, how the casual list-ener might easily be duped into believing that river-song remained the same for days on end until the floods came or the waters dropped in dry seasons to rock bottom. This was not the case at all he told them. There was a subtle difference every day guaranteed by the ever-changing flow. He explained how Gerry knew these things and he told how he himself could never pass a river without stopping to inspect the water and listen to the particular tune of the river in question. Afterwards the anglers went to their fav-ourite watering hole where they toasted the dead angler and drank their fill in his memory.

Noreen never attended the funeral. After a month she packed her bags and returned to England where she married a man who passed by a great river every day but never looked at it. That then is the sad tale of the Hermit of Scartnabrock who so unsuccessfully fished in the waters of matrimony but managed to land a few whoppers in the river of his dreams.

JOHNNY NAILE'S CHRISTMAS

It had always been Johnny Naile's ambition to play the role of Santa Claus. He had nearly succeeded once. He had the appropriate garments on. He hadn't put a drink to his lips all day. He had stayed indoors from four in the afternoon. He had shaved, washed, cut his toe-nails and then his finger-nails. He had trimmed his red beard and would have certainly been the only red-haired Santa Claus ever to be seen in the village of Cushnalicka.

Cushnalicka had its assortment of cottages and bungalows, forty in all, at either side of the road-way and there were two extra houses, the presbytery and the vicarage. The new vicar, a dapper figure, spare and lean and Church of Ireland, was smiling and pleasant which immediately made him suspect.

'Anyone,' the Catholic canon's housekeeper was fond of maintaining, 'who smiles non-stop isn't right in the head.'

The canon and parish priest of Cushnalicka and several surrounding townlands rarely smiled. Neither did his curate Fr Bressnan. 'He's too weak to smile', some of the less charitable of the Catholic parishioners were fond of saying when the curate's lack of condition would be the prevailing topic.

'Mrs Topp,' they would say maliciously, 'don't believe in feeding curates. Signs on they're never the same after a year or two in Cushnalicka.'

'It's a wonder to me,' said Hannah Toben, the schoolmaster's wife, 'that they don't fade away alto-

gether or collapse entirely or be capsized by a gale.'
When she spoke in this disparaging fashion she always made sure that there was no sign of Mrs Topp
in the vicinity.

Mrs Topp, a large, ambling, stern-faced widow
was the first to see Johnnie Naile as he attempted to
make his way unseen through what was once described
by a deceased postman as the most inquisitive resort
in Western Europe. Johnnie, in full regalia, was as inconspicuous as his parish priest in full canonicals on
Confirmation day. He was heartened as he drew near
the presbytery that there was no sign of the housekeeper but then, suddenly, she appeared with a sweeping brush in her hand in pursuit of a heretical tomcat
which had entered the sacred precincts without any
invitation whatsoever.

George Cudd, the local civic guard who was also
the only limb of the law in Cushnalicka, was heard to
say that those who credited cats with an understanding of human language weren't too far wrong. 'I mean,'
he confided to Mrs Toben, 'how else would the cat
hear that the presbytery was full of mice unless it was
a member of our species that let it drop.'

'They say,' Mrs Toben returned with equal confidentiality, 'that all the mice of the parish does have
their meetings there.'

'I've heard of stranger happenings,' the civic guard
nodded.

No sooner had Mrs Topp sent the tomcat about
his business than she uplifted her brush and intimated in no uncertain terms that the pathetic representation of Santa Claus which was defiling her pave-

ment was to come to a halt forthwith. Johnny Naile's apologetic smile revealed a mouthful of mixed molars, half of them as black as pitch and the remainder brown as hazelnuts. He was about to proceed on his way to the vicarage where he was expected when Mrs Topp confronted him a second time by forcing the head of the brush against his chest.

'I'll be late,' he pleaded. 'A promise is a promise missus.'

'A promise,' she called out to the street at large, 'sure no one would expect the likes of you to keep a promise.'

'This woman would,' he blurted out and suddenly covered his mouth with the palm of his right hand while he endeavoured to deliver a gentle hand-off with his free hand to the resolute housekeeper. The move made her all the more difficult to shift.

'You'd better make way for me woman because I'm comin' through,' Johnny shouted the warning while Mrs Topp braced herself.

Suddenly she changed her tack. Lowering the sweeping brush she forced a syrupy smile to her lips. Johnny Naile was more curious than disarmed. If Johnny's teeth were black and brown Mrs Topp's dentures were as white as snow but with the same tendency to shift. Shift they did with every word she spoke.

'Ah Johnny,' she was at her most cajoling now, 'be a good lad and tell me who the damsel is that you're meeting?'

'Can't do that missus,' Johnny was adamant.

Mrs Topp thrust a hand under his arm and endeavoured to guide him towards the front door of the presbytery which was still ajar after the cat's eviction.

'No, no, no missus,' Johnny held firm, 'what about the canon? What would he say if he caught me in the holy presbytery? I'd be excommunicated for sure with maybe jail on top of it.'

'The canon is gone to Limerick paying his sister her Christmas visit so you need have no fear of him. Come on now,' she wheedled and leaned her considerable rump against him to misdirect him indoors.

Johnny Naile realised that if he was to escape he would be obliged to knock the housekeeper to the ground and while he was reasonably sure that nothing would happen to her because of her abundant natural padding he could not be certain.

'Come on,' she whispered. 'I'll pour you a nice glass of the canon's very own whiskey the likes of which you never tasted in all your born days.'

At the mention of the word whiskey Johnny could not make up his mind whether to run or submit.

'One drop of whiskey won't do all that much harm,' he told himself.

As he stood hesitantly he remembered his promise to Mrs Trupple the vicar's wife. 'Wait until just after dark,' she told him, 'you'll find the hat and coat will fit nicely. You'll find the bag of gifts in the pantry. You'll find the back door will be open. All you have to do is push it in. We'll be in the living-room. You'll get your five shillings when the presents are handed over.'

'Is there boots with the outfit?' he asked.

'Those you have on will do nicely,' she assured him. Johnny looked downwards doubtfully at the turned-down wellingtons which were the only footwear in his possession. After her departure he went over her instructions and cursed himself repeatedly for not asking her to go over the instructions a few more times.

'And what the blazes was a pantry?' he asked himself. He solved that one by asking a passing schoolboy to enlighten him.

'A pantry is it?' the schoolboy had asked.

'Yes,' Johnny answered, 'a pantry. What exactly is a pantry?'

'Why,' said the schoolboy, 'a pantry is nothing only a bedroom.'

'Upstairs or downstairs?' Johnny asked.

'Upstairs of course you ignorant eejit,' the schoolboy called out as he ran off.

In the kitchen of the presbytery where he had allowed himself to be conducted, Johnny raised the canon's special whiskey to his lips and downed it in its entirety at one swallow.

'Another drop!' Mrs Topp poured a liberal dollop into the empty glass.

Again, because of fear of the canon and the unfamiliar surroundings, he swallowed the contents of the glass without taking it from his lips. A great sigh of satisfaction escaped him. If the first glass hit the spot then the second glass travelled all over so that a mighty shudder seized him and rocked him to the very tips of his toes.

'Relax,' Mrs Topp advised him as she directed him

towards a vacant chair. 'Now,' she demanded, 'what's that wan up to?'

'What wan?' Johnny asked drunkenly.

'Now,' said Mrs Topp as she held the snout of the bottle over his glass, 'will you be so good as to tell me the name of this damsel you're meeting?'

'Ah God help us,' said Johnny Naile, "tis no damsel. Sure 'tis only Mrs Trupple the vicar's wife.'

'Are you doin' Santa for her then?'

Johnny nodded and raised his glass to the snout. This time he divided the contents into two swallows. At the conclusion of the second he was visited by a deep drowsiness. Sensing that no further information was available and that there was a danger her visitor might fall asleep she assisted him to the door-way and sent him rollicking down the street in the general direction of the vicarage.

She had made an unwise investment. The scandal which she hoped would materialise out of Johnny's disclosures never did. She had long cherished the hope that something juicy would come her way and that she might bring that Trupple wan, as she called her, down a peg or two. What harm but she had been prepared, when the vicar and his wife first arrived, to let historical bygones be bygones and initiate the younger woman into the tricky rituals and formulas of village life. She had been prepared to take her under her wing despite the fact that she belonged to a different faith and spoke with a cultivated accent.

The young Mrs Trupple had not exactly ignored her. It would be truer to say that she simply wasn't aware of the older woman's standing in the community and tended to treat her the same as everybody else.

Mrs Topp saw herself as the leading female representative of the Catholic Church in the parish, as the third in command behind the canon and Fr Bressnan, the curate. She often felt disappointed that the Pope had never dubbed the housekeepers of the world's countless presbyteries with any sort of formal title. For instance, she frequently told herself, nuns are called sisters and high-up nuns are called reverend mothers and young nuns are called novices. But there was no title of any kind for the parochial housekeeper who carries responsibility for the entire parish and fills in for the parish priest in so many unseen ways and who often keeps wayward clerics on the straight and narrow. Even the young scallywags who serve Mass are called altar boys and the parish clerk has the finest title of all, that of sacristan.

Sacristan, she often repeated the title to herself. Wouldn't sacristaness be a nice name now! Sacristaness Topp! She imagined herself being introduced by a master of ceremonies on formal occasions such as an episcopal visit or wearing a black mantilla being conducted on a Vatican tour by a slender, dark-haired monsignor and then the final part of the proceedings with voluptuous organ music shutting out all other sounds followed by silence as she hears her name being called out in that sexy Italian accent: 'Your Holiness may I present to you the Sacristaness of Cushnalicka.'

She quickly reverted to reality and drew a coat over her shoulders before heading off in the direction of the vicarage. Johnny had obviously disappeared indoors or else had fallen into the road-side drain. She concealed herself beneath the shade of a large evergreen just across the road from the vicarage. The minutes passed and then a quarter-hour. She was about to depart when, unexpectedly, from an upstairs room across the road-way came a scream, loud, clear and terror-filled the way a good scream should be or so Mrs Topp felt. Other screams followed and then shouts and other alarms. Down the street came George Cudd, the civic guard, portly and ponderous and puffing like a steam engine, vainly endeavouring to pull up his trousers and button his tunic at the same time. He came to grief after a few steps but resolved both problems where he sat after his fall.

Mrs Topp rubbed her palms together in high glee. She choked a scream of pure, unbridled joy lest her presence be given away. The minutes passed and from the vicarage a large group emerged with Johnny Naile at the forefront, held firmly by George Cudd the civic guard and followed by the vicar and his wife and their three children.

Johnny Naile, deprived of his red coat and hat, was a sorry sight. Clad only in his shrunken vest and raggedy long johns and still possessed of his turneddown wellingtons he tried to explain his case but nobody would listen. George Cudd became so incensed with his proclamations of innocence that he kneed him forcefully several times in the behind. He even went so far as to draw his baton and threatened to use it if his prisoner continued with his vociferation. By this time a number of villagers had joined the motley assortment outside the vicarage.

'What's he done George?' asked Mrs Topp who had crossed from the other side to join the commotion.

'What hasn't he done?' George Cudd replied as he kneed his prisoner lest he make further protest-ations. George had just been joined by two precious if burly reinforcements in the shape of his wife Molly and her partly-deaf friend and neighbour Hannah Toben the schoolmaster's wife. Several adult topers from the village's two public houses joined the growing crowd. Blossom O'Moone wearing only her night-dress appeared in her doorway but did not join the throng. Blossom, according to numerous sources not all reliable, was the most accommodating girl in the village of Cushnalicka or for that matter in the entire parish or any other place you might care to name.

'But what will you be charging him with?' It was Mrs Topp again tugging at George Cudd's tunic.

'I'll be charging the wretch with attempted rape,' he informed those within earshot as he once more kneed his under-dressed prisoner, 'and I'll be charging him with resisting arrest and I'll be charging him with burglary.'

'What did he say?' Mrs Topp who was now out of earshot asked the person next to her who happen-ed to be Hannah Toben who happened to be hard of hearing at the best of time.

'He'll be charging him with buggery,' Hannah Toben replied in the exaggerated tone she used when she believed she was dealing with people who were as deaf as herself.

'Buggery.' The word carried to the outskirts of the crowd. Some laughed nervously. Others were shocked.

Buggery was something that happened elsewhere.

'String him up,' came a drunken call from behind a parked car pressed into service as a temporary latrine.

'Johnny Naile is a lot of things but he's no bugger and he's no rapist neither.' Blossom O'Moone it was who had spoken and after she made her views known there was silence the whole way to the barracks of the civic guards.

'What a story I'll have for himself when he comes back from his sister's!' The whispered words came from the thin lips of the Sacristaness of Cushnalicka. 'I won't say anything about the whiskey though and that's for sure,' she told herself.

Christmas morning presented itself without hail, rain or snow. The parishioners of Cushnalicka trooped to the earliest of the three Masses being celebrated on the sacred occasion. As always the canon was celebrant. Several years earlier he had resigned from a major parish in the south of the diocese. Unable for the heavy work-load and with an unprecedented shortage of priests he explained to the bishop that he would not retire. What he would like was a small parish, very small if possible, with just one curate to help him. The bishop had duly obliged with Cushnalicka which made everybody happy, especially Mrs Topp. Housekeeper to a priest was a fine thing but housekeeper to a canon with his tasselled hat and twenty or more scarlet buttons down the front of his soutane would make her the envy of the parish.

After Mass the congregation gathered in groups outside the church. The subject of conversation was the buggery and, of course, the attempted rape of the night before. The canon had only half listened as the housekeeper informed him of the terrible events that happened in his absence. As he was wont to do he doubted the veracity of all such tales and came to the conclusion that the housekeeper had been experimenting with his whiskey again. He never minded. She never took more than a glass or two and being a truly charitable man he concluded that she was as much entitled to the whiskey as he was provided she knew where to stop.

Despite the outrageous contents of his housekeeper's story he nevertheless took it upon himself to ring his friend the vicar. After the exchange of Christmas greetings and a promise to share a drink later in the day the vicar enlightened the canon regarding the events of the night before. Apparently when Johnny Naile arrived at the vicarage he was somewhat inebriated and mistook the master bedroom for the pantry.

The canon expressed no surprise. 'Johnny Naile,' he told the vicar, 'wouldn't know a pantry from a peashooter.'

Despite the fact that he was alcoholically incapacitated Johnny Naile made no noise as he entered the vicarage by the rear door and climbed the stairs to the master bedroom. Had he been wearing boots he would most certainly have been heard. Add to this the fact that the children were fast asleep having been out and about all day and would have dutifully pretended to be asleep anyway with the expectation of a visit from Santa Claus. The vicar had been preoccupied with his typewriter as he endeavoured to piece together a sermon for the following morning.

When Johnny arrived at the master bedroom he found the door open and the lights ablaze. Never before in his existence had he beheld such a bright and beautiful place. For a few hallucinatory moments he thought he might be in heaven but then he remembered the presents. Mrs Trupple had said they would be in the pantry and was not this the pantry! He tried high and low without success and then he was overcome by the heat of the place and by his exertions as well as the influence of three glasses of unwatered whiskey on an empty stomach. He fell across the large double bed and in a moment was fast asleep.

Alas, the vicar's wife lay reclining in her bath next door to the bedroom. Finishing her ablutions she rose and, totally oblivious to the happenings in the bedroom, entered that hallowed spot dragging a towel behind her and wearing only her birthday suit. The screams that followed were of a variety and pitch never before heard in the village of Cushnalicka. They were heard in every house. Those who slept were awakened and those who were awake wished they had been asleep. Prowling tomcats scurried into dark corners and the canines of the parish excelled themselves. The howling and the yowling would put a banshee to shame. Donkeys brayed in nearby fields and the moon raced for cover among the tattered clouds.

Johnny was released from custody just in time for last Mass on Christmas Day. He had no recall whatsoever of the previous night's events. The vicar had called earlier to the barracks and explained everything. George Cudd, having listened to his prisoner for most of the morning, had already deduced that he was holding an innocent man – if holding is the term for the solitary cell where Johnny was incarcerated was without a bolt or lock.

When Mass was over he was showered with offers of Christmas dinners for word had spread that he was innocent of all charges. The only offer he accepted was the one from Blossom O'Moone.

MACKSON'S CHRISTMAS

A enias Mackson, amiable as ever, kind and considerate, gave up his comfortable seat on the train. There were others who might have done so but they closed their eyes rather than look at the old lady with the large suitcase who had just come aboard. Christmas or no Christmas they had decided after they paid for their tickets that they would not surrender their seats on this occasion. Many would have done so in the past and felt that they had made their contributions, paid their dues so to speak and should be allowed to travel undisturbed, especially those going as far as Trallock one hundred and fifty miles down the line. Other male passengers who might have given in to the fragile figure so patently overburdened had varying reasons. Some would say that it was no concern of theirs, that if the old lady really wanted a seat she might have arrived earlier or travelled on the morning train.

One middle-aged man made an attempt to rise when she deposited her bag on the corridor by his side. He would have risen to his feet eventually. He had an elderly mother who had grown feeble in recent years and he wouldn't like to see her standing or so his conscience prompted him. He knew Aenias, had seen him several times in hotels and public houses in the city and would have laid a pound to a penny that he would volunteer his seat without a second thought. Not only did Aenias give up his seat to the old lady but he also saw to her luggage which consisted of the aforementioned suitcase and some small packages. Finding room for the suitcase presented problems as the overhead racks were already full. By removing his own smaller suitcase he managed to place the larger one, somewhat precariously, atop all the other luggage. In order to accomplish this he managed to stand on some toes and succeeded in brushing a lady's hat from her head.

'Do you mind!' she exclaimed in stentorian tones.

'That's my foot you know,' said the man on whose toe he had stepped unwittingly.

Aenias apologised profusely which was the only way he knew how to apologise. Having secured the old lady's possessions he found himself faced with another problem, the safe disposal of his own suitcase. The man with the toe pushed it down the corridor with his good foot as far as it could go and then firmly closed his eyes and folded his arms signalling his annoyance with Aenias.

'There's nothing in it,' this from the lady whose hat had fallen off. She lifted the suitcase and laughed as she announced its probable contents to her fellow passengers.

'More than likely a toothbrush,' she jibed and as she shook the case, 'a razor, possibly a bottle of hair oil or cream and a pair of sweaty socks I bet.'

Her remarks were greeted with laughter that was neither derisory nor hurtful. It was a Christmassy laughter. Aenias Mackson joined in while he rattled the suitcase good-naturedly as he made his way to the bar. He had promised himself earlier that day that he would avoid the bar on the journey down.

He had drunk his fill the night before and had spent the morning in a pub adjacent to the station loading up against the hang-over which the night had bequeathed him. He had promised his mother on the last occasion he had visited home that he would never arrive drunk again.

'I would rather,' she said tearfully, 'that you didn't come home at all.'

Well he wouldn't arrive home drunk this Christmas Eve. He would go to the train bar and nurse a few bottles of stout until he reached Trallock. He was well into his second bottle when the lady who had commented on his bag's contents entered.

'Are you going to buy me a drink?' she demanded.

'What would you like?' he asked gently.

'Gin and tonic,' she replied.

When he returned with the drink they located a place near the door-way.

'That man,' she said, 'on whose toe you stood made a pass at me.'

'Oh dear!' was all Aenias could say.

'Is that all you can say?' she asked. 'Anyway,' she continued, 'was I right about the contents of the bag?'

'More or less,' he answered. He did not tell her that while in the pub that morning he had opened the suitcase and in the true spirit of Christmas, as he might say himself, had given away the seasonal presents within to a poor family who had been occupying a nearby table when he had come in earlier. The presents were for two younger sisters and a brother at home in his native town and, of course, there was the headscarf for his mother. His father had died when Aenias was eight years old. He told his friends that he had never been the same afterwards.

'No matter what I do,' he confided to a friend, 'I'll never be the same. He was my world, my whole world.'

'A man who makes a pass at a girl he's never seen before this,' his new companion informed him, 'should be thrown off the train.'

As they sped towards Limerick City and then to his native Trallock she held his hand.

'The only reason I'm holding your hand,' she explained, 'is that I feel sullied after that man's pass at me. Well I suppose you could also say that I'm a little drunk and alone and maybe afraid too if the truth was told.'

They sat silently for awhile, neither anxious to shatter the repose their companionship had brought them.

'I have to go,' she said, 'Limerick's coming up.'

He rose when she did and walked with her to her seat where she recovered her bags and her coat. He took the bags in hand and made his way towards the exit.

'Will I see you again?' she smiled embarrassed by her courage.

'I hope so,' he answered.

'Have you got a biro?' she asked.

As he wrote her Dublin phone number on a slip of paper he spoke without raising his head. 'I hope you'll be in when I ring you,' he said.

'If I'm not,' she said, 'you must ring again and

again.' Then she was gone.

He found a vacant seat and a place for his suitcase and drifted into an uneasy slumber from which he did not waken until he arrived in Trallock. He looked at his watch. 'Time for another drink.'

His mother never went to bed before midnight. His sisters and brother would be awake expecting him. Despite many lapses over several Christmases their faith in him never wavered.

In a downtown pub he joined with a party of friends from his boyhood. After midnight had passed he reminded himself that he should go home. He was fully aware of the pattern into which he was falling. It was exactly the same as the past several Christmases. He was forced to admit that while he had a shilling in his pocket he was a compulsive avoider of home and family. He knew that his relationship with his mother was on the line and yet when he was asked by his friends if he was having another drink he confirmed that he was. He often asked himself if he was an alcoholic but he would always provide himself with reassuring answers. He could, for instance, go off the juice any time he wanted. He was popular with his friends. He had a good job in the Department of Industry and Commerce. His superiors had no complaints to make about him. Okay, so he owed a few pounds. He owed money to his mother. Frantically he searched his pockets. The presents which he had purchased and given away had taken their toll on his finances; so had the drinks he purchased.

In recall he realised that nobody had brought him a single drink all day, not until now. His needless extravagance with total strangers had left him with no more than a few pounds. Thank God he had purchased a return ticket. He remembered one very large order for which he had paid that morning in the pub near the station. A group of friends had joined his poor people at the next table. Introductions followed and he found himself paying for their drinks. He had been shocked at the price but he had insisted despite the protestations of the recipients. Phrases like 'ah you're too decent!' and 'he has a heart o' gold' started to drift back to him through the alcoholic excitement of the morning. Now he was left with a single £5. Aenias had £80 starting out. He might not be an alcoholic but he was without doubt a wanton spendthrift. It would have to stop. He recalled the previous Christmas when his mother discovered he was broke and that this was the reason he stayed in bed over the holiday.

'I'm not being hard on you Aeney,' she told him, 'there's no need when you're so hard on yourself. You're just like your father, spending all you have on strangers and no thought for your own. How nice it would be for your brother and sisters if you took them to the pictures. If you had a car you could take us all for a drive.'

He had laughed bitterly but inwardly at this. A car! That was rich when he couldn't even afford a bicycle. The man behind the bar counter was calling time. Aenias looked at his watch. Mother o' God! Five o'clock in the morning! Where did the hours go! All victims of the season he told himself the same as his money. As he walked home with his suitcase rattling he insisted to the stars overhead that he was just a creep. He found the key of the front door and tiptoed upstairs to bed. There was no sound in the house.

Later when he woke it was still dark but his watch told him that it was the darkness of the afternoon of Christmas Day. Why had nobody alerted him! The least they might have done was to call him for the Mass or for his Christmas dinner. Downstairs his brother and sisters assured him that they had called him repeatedly but that he had been in a stupor every time. They placed his Christmas dinner in front of him. It was still hot but the pain in his head saw off his appetite. He pecked at the food and asked about his mother. When he didn't wake she had rented a cab and gone to her sister in the country. She might not return for a few days. She had not been feeling well. They were careful to lay no blame on him.

He told them how he had agonised about their presents and that he had no money either. He was truly ashamed of himself but they gathered round him and told him they loved him. They still had their Christmas monies, presents from neighbours, from aunts, uncles and cousins, dollars from America and English pounds galore. They heaped it upon him and to give him his due he faithfully recorded every penny he borrowed. The fact that he already owed them never entered the picture. In a few weeks he assured them he would repay every penny. He would go off the drink and he would never embarrass anybody again, particularly at Christmas. They told him he never embarrassed anybody in his life and that the money they gave him was a gift and that he was to forget about it.

They went for a walk round the deserted town stopping at each of the three churches to visit the sacred cribs where the infant Jesus lay, serenely, in his cot. The sisters Rita and Fiona, fifteen and fourteen, linked arms to their older brother throughout while Tom, the younger brother, brought up the rear. After an hour they returned to the family home where Aenias managed to finish most of the turkey and stuffing he had been unable to stomach earlier. Afterwards the foursome played cards and still later Aenias regaled them with city tales, largely humorous but sometimes unbearably sad. As the night wore on Aenias began to look at his watch with increasing regularity. His listeners guessed that his anxiety for drink was getting to him.

'Why don't you two go for a drink?' the older sister suggested to the brothers.

'Well now,' said Aenias with a chuckle, 'that would be the very last thought in my head.'

'Me too,' Tom put in, 'but if my mother finds out life won't be worth living for the rest of the year.'

'There's nobody here going to tell her,' Fiona assured him, 'provided of course ...' and she left the phrase hanging as Aenias looked speculatively from one sister to the other.

'Provided what?' he asked.

'Well,' Fiona explained reluctantly. 'He puked into the kitchen sink the last time and never cleaned up.'

'I promise I won't ever again do that,' Tom assured her. 'I was green then.'

'Of course you were.' Aenias clapped him on the back. 'I puked in the kitchen sink myself when I was seventeen and you can be sure that very few sinks have escaped a good puke at this time of the year.

'What time will you be back?' the younger sister asked.

'We'll be back in an hour at the outside,' Aenias promised.

'We'll wait up then,' the older sister's tone carried a trace of uncertainty. As the brothers left Aenias kissed both sisters and promised he would be as good as his word but again the pattern remained unchanged except that Tom had more than enough by the time midnight came round. Aenias would follow much later. He fell in with his companions of the previous night. They were pleased to see him. Those in big groups who failed to buy their rounds eventually found themselves isolated. It had been an established fact for years that Aenias always saw to his round and generally bought more than his share. Aenias left the premises where he had spent seven consecutive hours at six o'clock on the morning of St Stephen's Day or the Wren's Day as they still called it in the locality.

Aenias did not rise on the following day. The same dull headache assailed him when he awakened at noon. He declined all offers of food or drink and fell into a deep sleep from which he did not wake until nine o'clock that night. He missed the colourful wren boys' bands with their spotless white uniforms, their tinselly, peaked caps and their painted moustaches as well as all the traditional singing and dancing for which they were justly famous.

Aenias crept round the room on tiptoe and located his trousers. He searched the pockets and found only a handful of silver. The pockets of his coat were not nearly as productive. He went back to bed. He could not face the group, who would surely be in the public house by now, without the price of a round at least. He realised that his brother and the girls were waiting downstairs but he did not have the heart to face them. Filled with self-loathing he reminded himself for the umpteenth time since he came home that he was nothing more than a creep.

'I'm gone beyond redemption,' he said in a whisper, 'and that's a terrible thing to say at Christmas.'

He woke several times during the night. It was still dark when he started to get ready for the train. As he shaved he winced at the smell of rashers frying downstairs. He prayed that his mother would be still away. Hardly home yet he told himself. She would have confronted him already. He could have spent another day at home, even two days but his time had come. No money and no zest and no hope.

He put on a brave face as he went downstairs. He rushed out to the back kitchen when he beheld the enormous display on his plate. It was colourful as it was plentiful with cubes of black and white puddings, sausages nicely browned, a little burning here and there which was the way he liked them. He didn't deserve such sisters. Then there were tomatoes in abundance each sliced into equal parts and liver. Where the blazes did they get the liver on a holiday morning and at such an hour! Gently he embraced sisters and brother, relishing their healthy appetites as he tinkered with the toast for which he had asked.

At the station the four Macksons stood dejectedly together. Aenias leaned over and whispered to Tom. 'I am the sole owner,' he said, 'of the worst headache any man ever had.'

'I'll pray for you,' Tom whispered back. 'From now on I'll pray for you all the time.

'Pray for me!' Aenias was about to laugh but then it came back to him, something his mother had told him one day that last Christmas they spoke together. 'Tom's teachers believe he has a vocation for the priesthood,' she had told him proudly.

As they moved towards the train which had silently entered the station Aenias whispered a second time to his brother. 'I could do with a few prayers,' he said. He found himself shivering uncontrollably as the sisters handed him the suitcase. He felt like a man deserted and degraded as they stepped backwards, their eyes brimming with tears. The suitcase contained infinitely more on its return journey. There was a heavy pull-over and a shirt from his mother, socks, underwear and towels from his sisters and *The Oxford Book of Irish Verse* from Tom.

THE GREATEST WAKE OF ALL

Sam Toper always looked forward to Christmas. Sam's wife and family did not. Sam looked forward to Christmas because it was a time of free drinks. If one chanced to be in the right bar at the right time one was always sure to meet merry old gentlemen and, indeed, younger gentlemen who insisted in buying drinks for all and sundry. They would even buy drinks for people they had never before seen in all their lives. Sam couldn't understand it but because it was beneficial to him he totally accepted it. You wouldn't have any business explaining the spirit of Christmas to Sam and need I add that expressions like 'peace and goodwill' or 'come all ye faithful' would be meaningless to him.

Down deep he understood that there was an inexplicable chemistry at work, a chemistry which ordained that stingy oul' codgers who otherwise would not give him the time of day were prepared to press free drink on him at this particular time of year. If you were to suggest to Sam that he might more fully enter into the spirit of things if he himself bought drinks for people who were worse off than he was, Sam would be certain to double over in convulsions of laughter. From the look on his face after the laughter had subsided you would gather that it was one of the more preposterous proposals he had ever heard. Those who knew Sam well such as his wife and family and, of course, his neighbours were all agreed that Sam was a lousy creep, that he would not give you the itch if he had nine doses of it and that the idea of returning a favour was nothing short of reprehensible.

His employer, one Bustler Hearne, would have sacked him immediately after taking him on but for the fact that he could get no one else to work for him. Bustler Hearne was a bully and had beaten the daylights out of most of his previous employees for heinous crimes such as being late five minutes on wet mornings or for suggesting a rise in wages. It must however, be taken into account that nobody else would employ Sam Toper because they couldn't motivate him the way Bustler could.

Bustler's business consisted of plucking and trussing fowl, particularly geese and turkeys, during the run up to Christmas. For weeks before he would purchase his Christmas requirements from the fowl-rich countryside within a radius of ten miles. Of his regular employees, a Miss Dotie Tupper aged eighty-four was in charge of cash sales and another, our friend Sam, was fowl dispatcher and plucker-in-chief. Extra staff were taken on during the Christmas period. There was no such structure as a regular wage. One was paid for the number of turkeys plucked in the round of a day and woe betide the man or woman who damaged birds while plucking.

Sam was a model plucker when he put his mind to it and because he was possessed of an insatiable appetite for pints of stout he plucked like a man possessed, often earning three times as much as ordinary pluckers. Sam's wife Moya and their seven children had no great regard for Christmas. They loved their mother and each other after a fashion but because

Christmas had never been kind to them they were never generous in their praise of it. There was no scarcity of food. The requisite share of Sam's weekly wage was put aside for Moya and would be collected by one of the older children when it fell due. Sam kept the balance so that he might satisfy his outrageous thirst.

'If,' said Canon Coodle the well beloved parish priest, 'there is even a solitary half-penny missing from Moya's share of your wages I will raise you aloft and turn you inside out after which I will truss you and singe you and cast you into the depths of the quarry.' It mattered not to Canon Coodle that there was no water in the quarry hole nor had there ever been. It was the way he used his deep voice that made the hair stand on Sam's head.

There was another reason why the young Topers had no great affection for Christmas. They were constrained by their father to work as part-time goose and turkey pluckers during the Christmas holidays when other youngsters were roving the countryside in search of holly and ivy for the family cribs. They were made to work from dawn till dark and deprived of their rightful wages by their drink-crazed father. It was too late when Sergeant Ruttle heard about it but when he did he presented Sam with three deep and accurate kicks on his booze-fattened posterior and threatened him with life imprisonment if such a malpractice ever occurred again.

After that the children started to enjoy Christmas especially when Canon Coodle found them suitable employment for a few days before Christmas. The money would be spent on inexpensive gifts before their father found out about it and demanded that it be handed over so that he might slake his unquenchable thirst.

When the three older children arrived into their middle and late teens they made contact with aunts and uncles in England and the United States and eventually wound up in New York where they found gainful employment. They would save most assiduously from their very first wage packet with a view to bringing the entire family, father excluded, to New York where they might start life afresh.

Naturally the three eldest went first. They kept their departure a secret from their father. When he found out he locked the remainder of the family out for several nights. They found refuge with neighbours until Sergeant Ruttle was informed. On this occasion, although by no means a violent man, the sergeant doubled the number of posterior kicks normally implanted. Afterwards Sam took a pledge against drink which lasted for twenty-four hours.

Life went on and then an elderly neighbour died. He was one of two brothers, pint-sized cobblers who eked out the most meagre of existence's in a tiny, one-storeyed house five doors up the lane-way from the Toper abode. People who came with shoes to be repaired had difficulty in telling the brothers apart. They were aged seventy and seventy-one, always slept in the same bed, never argued, were invariably kind to each other and never missed eight o'clock morning Mass in St Mary's church in the centre of the town. Let there be hail, rain or thunder, let there be sleet, snow or storm the brothers faced the elements each morning with happy faces and cheerful hearts.

The Toper children spent much of their spare time during the winter months huddled around the diminutive peat fire in the cobblers' shop listening to the many folktales which had been passed on from generation to generation and which now reposed in the fabulous memory of the compact cobblers of Cobblers' Lane for it was by this name that the lane was known.

All would change in a few short years. The last of the cobblers passed on to that happy clime where wax and heelball, thongs and laces were as plenteous as the green grass on the lush pastures of planet earth and where the shining steel of lasts and awls lighted the surrounds as far as the eye could see. People no longer slept on straw mattresses and there would be no more fleas. Urban councils everywhere would provide sturdy homes with baths and toilets and sufficient rooms for modern families. But there would always be people who would look askance at houses for the poor, holidays for the poor, subsistence for the poor and enough to eat for the poor.

The cobblers of Cobblers' Lane went by the names of Mickey and Mattie Mokely. It was Mattie who died one night in his sleep. When Mickey felt the cold form he knew that something was amiss. He called his brother gently by his name and when that failed to elicit a response he tapped him gingerly on the shoulder. He slapped him on the back but there was no reaction so he rose from the bed and lighted a candle which he held under Mattie's nose and then under Mattie's mouth but not the least flicker did the flame design.

The younger brother donned his clothes for now there was irrefutable proof that his brother was dead. As soon as he was dressed he bent over his brother's ear and recited the final act of contrition. Then he called the neighbours, one of whom went for the doctor while two went for the priest because it was the custom that a lone man or woman should never go for the priest unless there was no one else available. It was believed that a lone person might be more susceptible to the wiles of the devil and might be diverted from the presbytery where the priest was always available. Old people would recount instances where loners were found drowned in nearby rivers and streams while others fell foul of unseasonal mists and were tumbled inexplicably down precipices and into crevices where they might be found many years later or not found at all. On the other hand a pair of stout men with goodwill in their hearts and rosary beads wrapped round their fingers were known to be proof against all evil.

Despite the poverty of the times Mattie Mokely was waked well with three different varieties of whiskey, with port, sherry and rum, with Dutch gins and imported snuff. If memory serves me correctly I remember once to have overheard that vodka had yet to make its presence felt in the lanes and streets of Ireland. Mattie was laid out in his Sunday best. This consisted of his Clydesdale-blue suit, his low shoes or slippers as they were called. These had the brightness of polished ebony thanks to the ministrations of Mrs Hanlon, Canon Coodle's housekeeper. She admitted afterwards that she would perform such a chore for nobody else – the canon excepted.

'Mattie Mokely,' said she, 'was always a gentleman and I would be remiss if I didn't send him shining to the gates of heaven.'

During the wake, food was handed round. All would be paid for without fail when the obsequies were over and every penny would come from the life-savings of the Mokelys. Seven pigs' heads boiled almost to jelly were sliced and sent upon the rounds. There was ham, lamb, ram and jam the neighbours boasted afterwards. There were barm bracks and seed loaves and home-made scones by the score all provided by generous neighbours to whom the Mokely brothers would have shown kindnesses over the years. Credit was always extended to the hard-up and no one went without a pair of half-soles just because he was temporarily penniless. In spite of this there was little or nothing owing to the Mokely brothers. Only one man abused their generosity and failed to meet his commitments. That man you know already but his wife and family would do their best in the course of time to cancel his debts.

Sam's wife and family were held in high regard by all who knew them whereas no one was held in lower regard than Sam and yet it was the very same Sam who, in the early stages of the wake, consumed three times as much whiskey as anybody else and who, may God forgive all gluttons, devoured two heaped plates of pigs' head, plates which were destined for other folk who were too considerate to look after themselves. When Sam had eaten his fill and drank his nuff he retired for a few hours to his abode where he stretched himself on his bed so that he might be prepared later on in the night for a second assault on the booze and comestibles.

Many people in Cobblers' Lane and further afield had predicted for years that Sam would have a bad end, that he would simply burst one day and that would be the end of him. Dr Matt Coumer knew better. Once when Sam had a drunken fall and needed some stitches the doctor, without Sam's consent, conducted a thorough check on this money-on candidate for a speedy demise. Matt was amazed by his findings which he passed on to none save a few select colleagues. Blood samples had been taken, pulse and blood pressure checked and re-checked, heart and lungs exhaustively recorded for flaw or failure but at the end of the day Matt was obliged to concede that for his age, weight and de-bauched habits Sam was the nonpareil of the local medical scene.

While the wake continued unabated Sam slept soundly and snored not at all. It was the practise of the period for poor people to set aside money on a regular basis for a decent wake and funeral lest they be disgraced in the eyes of the world. They would be able to say afterwards that they had met their obligations. 'We waked him well,' they would say or, 'we waked him dacent God be good to him.'

They would see to it that none of the mourners left the house in a sober state or with an empty stomach. To this end Mickey Mokely had spent every last shilling of his and his brother's savings. It never occurred to Mickey that should he pass on prematurely there would be little or nothing left to pay for his wake and funeral. The county council, of course, would provide enough

122

to pay for a coffin and he would be in a position to share a free grave courtesy of his brother but there would be no drink and there would be no food. The way Mickey saw it was that he would survive long enough to put aside the cost of a decent wake and funeral for himself.

As the night wore on the more magnanimous grew the tributes to the dead man. These would be forthcoming anyway whether the deceased was a good man or not. They cost nothing and it brought some degree of consolation to the relatives. The praise came mostly from the elderly female neighbours who sat near the death bed. With nodding heads they counted their beads between glasses of sherry or port. The ritual recital would go on for hours. When one group had exhausted their superlatives, another group would take over.

The words of praise had replaced the lonely keening which dominated such proceedings from time immemorial. The keeners were drawn from certain families who were held to be more professional than genuine mourners who might let down the side by not crying at all, who would be too stunned by the loss to give vent to any sound save an anguished sighing which could hardly be heard. Others would be too shy or too backward while others still were too heart-broken. There were more who felt that prayer heaped upon gentle prayer for hours on end was the appro-priate method of mourning. The keeners had nothing against prayer. What was keening after all but a form of chanted or sung prayer! True professional keeners would shed tears when ever required and assume facial expressions so tragic that the very sight of them would trigger off fountains of tears from over-crowded wake rooms. Some cynical mourners would argue that it was no bother at all to cry when one's gut was filled with whiskey or wine but the truth was that these were exceptional women and in the old days a wake without their ilk was like a bastable without a bottom.

As the night drifted into morning at the Mokely wake people began to drift away to their homes so that when the hour of one struck only a handful remained. These, for the most part, would have been immediate neighbours, one or more of whom would be expected to sit up with the corpse until morning when the normal activities of the lane and nearby streets resumed.

One of the last groups to leave the wake-room was the Toper family which consisted of Moya and her four children. They made their goodbyes to Mattie and went out into the night. They tiptoed silently downwards to their home where the head of the family was just beginning to stir having spent three hours of unbroken sleep in his bed and might well had spent several more had he not been awakened by the cold of his own waters which would not be restrained such was the earlier intake of liquor by their proprietor. He hurried from the little back room where he generally slept alone only to be confronted by his family who happened to be entering the house as he was leaving it. He issued a stern lecture about late hours and cuffed the children. As Moya passed hurriedly inwards she drew a kick at her but he was caught off balance and fell out on to the street where small clusters of mourners were still gathered. Smiling benignly at those who spared him a glance he increased his normal gait to a frantic run lest all the wake-room liquor be consumed.

His fears were groundless. The wake-room was empty and all he could see was the corpse clad in his Clydesdale and good shoes. He immediately lifted a whiskey bottle to his head and sought around for a bottle of stout which would serve as a chaser. He was delighted to see that a full crate of bottled stout occupied an honoured position under the death bed. He would guard it with his life as he would the mortal remains of Mattie. As he sat a handful of neighbours silently entered, looked around, smiled knowingly and made no comment. They would return later and dutifully perform their stint by the corpse.

Sam ignored them and was pleased to observe that they had not interfered with the crate beneath the bed. There was many a man of proven courage and many a truly pious man who would face a raging bull rather than sit alone with a corpse. For Sam, however, the remains beside him on the death bed presented no problem. Mattie had presented no threat in life and should therefore present even less of a threat in death. Anyway Sam was never a man to be intimidated by the hereafter or by the thought of the hereafter or so he said himself. His only fear in life was that some disaster might befall the world and close down the breweries and distilleries thereby leaving him threatened by the long thirst which he had always feared.

'As long as I have a bottle of stout in my hand,' he once declared to a neighbour, 'I have no fear of the hereafter or the hereunder but as little. Let 'em come at me sideways or downways or upways and you'll find me standing my ground. You can keep your guns and your swords and put a bottle of whiskey by my side, preferably a bottle of ten-year old Jameson and we'll see who'll come out on top.'

He drank contentedly for an hour and then he recalled the offspring who had reduced his income by high-tailing it to the United States. He never made vocal threats when he was alone. Instead he liked to growl at the absent faces of those he believed to have wronged him. People who had been privy to this growl would declare afterwards that they had never heard a sound like it, that it resembled nothing on the face of the earth. They would solemnly swear that no animal, domestic or wild, was capable of such spine chilling utterances.

Dr Matt Coumer once heard the very same sounds emanating from the local grave-yard on a fine summer's night as he rambled through the suburbs with his wife. She had stopped dead and would not budge an inch. Matt would be the first to admit that he was not the bravest man in the community but he allowed his curiosity to get the better of him. Assuring his wife that there was nothing to fear he followed his ears to the horrific noises. After a brief search he noticed the human form rolled up against the side of an ancient tomb.

'I was reminded of Shakespeare,' Matt informed his friend the Badger Loran with whom he was drinking in the back lounge of Crutleys. 'You remember the ghost in *Hamlet*,' Matt recalled.

'Why wouldn't I?' responded the Badger, who had never even heard of *Hamlet* not to mind the ghost.

'You remember where the ghost describes the secrets of his prison house?'

'Course I do,' the Badger answered with a wink at Mrs Crutley.

'How's that it goes again?' Matt pondered. 'Ah yes indeed. I have it now,' and he went on to quote the relevant lines:

> 'would harrow up thy soul, freeze thy young blood,
> make thy two eyes, like stars, start from their spheres,
> thy knotted and combined locks to part,
> and each particular hair to stand on end,
> like quills upon the fretful porpentine.

'Well that's exactly how I felt my friend as I studied the crumpled heap of humanity before my eyes. At first I thought it must be a bear which had some how escaped from a distant zoo but I had second thoughts and realised that it must be some truly formidable member of the ape family. I was about to depart and report the sighting to my friend Sergeant Bill Ruttle but then the creature leaped to its feet and looked me between the eyes. I wouldn't give tuppence for my life at that moment but then I noticed the face and the unmistakable whiff of stale whiskey. The creature had stopped sounding off at this stage. It was when the growling stopped that I knew who stood before me. It was the one and only Sam Toper. When he recognised me he resumed his former position and commenced his out-pourings once more.'

Matt admitted to the Badger that he was utterly overcome by laughter. He hurried to the grave-yard gate and informed his nervous wife of all he saw and heard. She accompanied him to the tomb where Sam had changed his position and was now sitting on his behind with his head resting on his knees. The awesome growling still continued. Matt and his wife laughed loud and long and indeed laughed loud and long for many nights afterwards.

As Sam sat near the death bed he thought he heard a sound coming from that unlikely place. He took no notice and re-addressed himself to the bottle of whiskey. After a goodly swallow he felt the pangs of hunger assailing his whiskey-drenched saliva. He stumbled around the wake-room in search of suitable sustenance. A milder growl escaped him. It was a growl of satisfaction for he had located an unfinished plate of pig's head. He devoured it like a starving lion, grunting and gasping as he did. Then and not till then did the corpse sit up on the death bed.

At first Sam could not believe what he saw. He placed the pig's head and the whiskey on the ground and rubbed his eyes. He had often been confronted by strange apparitions before but he had always been able to trace them to the excessive consumption of whiskey.

'I'm not that drunk,' he told himself, 'so it can't be whiskey.'

Slowly he took his knuckles from his eyes. The corpse was now sitting on the side of the bed and it was speaking.

'What's the hour Sam?' the corpse asked politely.

Sam replied with an ear-splitting scream. Other

screams and assorted spasms followed as he bounded over the death-bed and disappeared into the starry night.

'Save me, save me!' he called pitifully.

Outside awaiting their turn to sit up with the corpse were the three neighbours who had entered earlier. They made no move for they could see nobody from whom Sam might be saved.

'Save me. Save me,' he shouted as he ran through his own front door knocking it from its rusty hinges. He ended up under his bed and did not reappear until Mattie was safely buried later in the day.

It would be some time before the truth emerged. Shortly before the figure sat up on the bed Sam had stolen forty winks. While he snoozed, the corpse's brother, Mickey, found himself unable to resist the advances of sleep. Too much drink added to extreme physical exhaustion had driven him into a trance-like state so he did what he always did. He drew back the clothes and lay in the bed beside his brother. After a short while he felt the chill. With a few heaves and pushes he succeeded in dumping the corpse on to the floor. Mickey dropped off and slept for two hours by which time the intrepid Sam had instituted his search for suitable nourishment.

After the funeral an air of gloom hung over the lane-way. Most of the houses were left in darkness out of respect to the dead man. After a few days the pall lifted. Mickey re-opened his shop and was visited on an hourly basis by the neighbours. They brought him broth and they brought him pies and they brought him pancakes in their turn. One or more sat with him all day long and little by little he began to accept the sad fact that he would face the remainder of his life alone. Neighbours were fine and neighbours cared but in the last analysis neighbours had other priorities.

Nobody ever told the true story to Sam Toper. All concerned came to the conclusion that he was better off the way he was. It would be wrong to say that he wasn't the same after his experience but it would be true to say that minor changes occurred in the years that followed. He stopped kicking Moya for one thing. All he did now was slap her face and throw the occasional punch at her midriff. Other times he would rise from his couch in the middle of the night when the injustices he had suffered over a life-time surfaced and prevented him from going to sleep. After a spell of teeth-grinding and other rasping noises from mouth and throat he would commence his growling. He would never enter her room which she shared with the children. He would reduce himself to all fours outside her bedroom door and embark upon a long and highly varied session of hostile natterings and intimidatory mutterings. These were but the prelude to the spine-chilling snarls and warning snorts which were at the very centre of Sam's discontent. Moya and the children generally slept throughout unless, in a specially malignant fit of pique after too much liquor, he might throw the entire family out into the street. Almost immediately one of the neighbours would alert Sergeant Bill Ruttle who shepherded the family back indoors after which he never failed to implant several stinging bone-shaking kicks on Sam's rear. These worked wonders with the temperament of Sam and never failed to reduce his growling to pitiful sobs and whimpers.

Bill took it upon himself to enlist the remaining boys of the Toper family in the Trallock boxing club. At fifteen and fourteen respectively Fiachra and Conn Toper were regarded as likely prospects although the sergeant never intimated that they should one day use their skills against their bullying father unless, of course, in self-defence.

Sam was the kind of fighter who, if he knew he was capable of defeating an opponent, would beat him senseless whereas he would run a mile from a better man. One might be tempted to ask why a better man or men were never called in to balance the situation. It was chiefly because there was an unwritten law at the time that the head of the household was the unquestioned master of his domain. Fine if Bill booted him around now and then but for a layman to intervene would amount to an invasion of the home and the home above all other things was regarded as sacred by Church and State. Then there was the awful prospect that Sam might be injured or even killed if the security of his home was breached. Who would provide for his wife and family and who would pay for his funeral?

Sam survived and never changed his tyrannical ways. Time passed and a white Christmas presented itself for the dazzlement and delight of young and old. There had not been a white Christmas in the parish of Trallock for nine years. The flakes arrived first in faint flurries and rarely alighted on the ground.

Instead they drifted around the streets and lane-ways moving slowly westward and increasing slowly in density all the time. Four days before the great feast the snow began to come down in real earnest, whitening the roof-tops and the surrounding fields, brightening the hearts of the young folk and recalling for the older people happy days of childhood when somehow the snow never seemed as cold. Then, just three days before Christmas a great event took place. A tall handsome man well-dressed and well-made alighted from the mid-day train at Trallock railway station. Immediately he commissioned two local bag carriers to take charge of his luggage which was considerable. He preceded the pair to the town centre where he entered the town's only travel agency. When his business was concluded he instructed his carriers to follow him to the poorest quarter of the town. The carriers showed no surprise. Often over the years and especially as Christmas drew near they would have been hired by well-off strangers to transport luggage to unlikely destinations. The lone strangers, it invariably transpired, would have been local men who had made good abroad, especially in England and America and occasionally in Australia. All these successful homecomers represented only a very small percentage of those who were forced to emigrate in the first place. Not everybody succeeded in their places of exile and not everybody who did remembered to come home.

As the party arrived at the corner which led to Cobblers' Lane they were ambushed by a cheerful party of snowballing youths and children who had grown tired of snowballing each other. The tall young man returned fire and instructed his carriers to do likewise. There followed a joyful exchange of snowballs which goes to show, if it ever needed showing, that bag carriers as well as visiting gentlemen are all children at heart. A man who does not know this, as Canon Cornelius Coodle might say, knows very little.

The four unexiled Toper siblings who were at the head and tail of the ambush went by the names of Fiachra, Conn, Aedh and Fionnuala which were the names of the Children of Lir, the great mythical sea god who married Aobh and had three sons and a daughter who were changed into swans by Lir's second wife Aoife. It was Mental Nossery the poet who suggested the names to Moya after the poet had found her wandering in tears round Trallock grave-yard with marks on her face, one summer's morning a few weeks before she gave birth to her fourth child. The child was called Fiachra.

It was Fionnuala, the youngest of the Toper children, who recognised the tall handsome young man. When he followed her and lifted her in the air she screamed and then smiled when she saw the laughing face of her oldest brother Frank. Great rejoicings followed but these were eclipsed by the total joy of Frank's revelations that he had tickets to New York for his mother and the four other members of the family. All were sworn to secrecy for the good reason that Sam would be within his rights to prevent his younger children from leaving home before they reached legal age. When Sam arrived home late that evening he was partially covered in feather and turkey droppings. He acknowledged Frank's presence with a grunt but then realising that Frank would surely be well heeled he invited him out for a drink. Drink was the last thought in Frank's head but he agreed. His father needed to be humoured lest he deduce that he was being duped for the second time. In the public house Sam Toper called for a glass of whiskey and a pint bottle of stout.

'Pay for that!' he instructed his oldest son.

More drinks followed, all paid for by Frank. Sam drank his fill and almost slept out the following morning which would never do, he reminded himself, with hundreds of turkeys and geese still waiting to be plucked and no wages forthcoming until the bare pelts were singed and trussed. He gulped down a cup of tea and rushed out the door to his place of employment. If he was a solitary minute late he would be docked an hour's wages by the eighty-four year old timekeeper Dotie Topper who, according to all the employees under her supervision, could see around corners and had eyes in the back of her head as well as an ear-splitting bell which sounded off when ever the only door to the plucking quarter was opened.

When Sam returned home for his lunch at one o'clock the first thing he noticed was the cold and the second was the absence of any form of appetising odour such as that of beef stew or bacon and cabbage or roast chicken. All cockerels and pullets badly damaged in the plucking were available to staff at half price and there would be many of these at Christmas. Sam's suspicions were aroused when he finally became aware of the profound silence. He hurried through the house calling out his wife's name and then the names of the children. Panting he ran out the door and never slackened his pace until he reached the railway station. Its only occupants were the pair who carried his son's suitcases to Cobblers' Lane the previous afternoon. Their lines were carefully rehearsed, their stories convincing. Yes! The children and the mother had all boarded the Dublin-bound passenger train at half-past nine that morning. Sam hurried to the barracks where he was interviewed by Sergeant Bill Ruttle. He demanded the return of his children without delay. He threatened the sergeant with legal proceedings which could cost him his job if he didn't get a move on. Bill guessed that the Topers were by now on their way by bus from Limerick city to Shannon airport. Later he would question friends and neighbours in Cobblers' Lane.

The children had looked elegant in the new clothes Frank had brought with him from New York and the neighbours would swear in any court of law that a more contented group of people never left Cobblers' Lane. Sam did not die of a broken heart. He did not love his children and he did not love his wife. The only person he loved was Sam. He questioned the neighbours but they had seen nothing, heard nothing and were too busy in the first place, minding their own business.

As time passed Sam began to come to terms with his loss. He had extra money for drink and he lived out of tins. Sardines, beans and bread and butter were his basic diet. He thrived but his growling had entered a new phase. He now betook himself to the grave-yard for a few hours every evening. It afforded him the isolation he needed to indulge in his now demented growling activities. On the rare occasions when he was visited by outlandish urges he would climb on the flat roof of an ancient tomb and hold forth loudly and at length, slobbering and whining, pillalooing and yelping sometimes savagely and sometimes gently. All his complaints were directed at his absent family.

Then a surprising development took place. He began to attract the attention of dogs. These were, for the most part, good-natured mongrels who indulged him and who followed him around in the hope that he might unearth something out of the ordinary. In time they ignored him but there still remained a few disciples who trailed him when they had nothing better to do. Alas one day while he held forth from an all-fours position on a large limestone flag at the farthest corner of the grave-yard he found himself confronted by two vicious Alsatians who savaged him beyond recognition for having the temerity to growl at them. They had returned to the town after an unsuccessful sheep search in the nearby hills. Well known for their murderous onslaughts a look-out had spotted them as they passed through a large upland field. The look-out had raised the alarm and in a short while several armed sheep farmers appeared on the scene. The killers, however, with that particular canine cunning common to sheep killers had disappeared. The grave-yard had proved on occasion to be a source of food. Lazy, uncaring vandals from the locality would dump occasional carcasses over the grave-yard wall in the dead of night. Chiefly these would be aborted calves or dead cats and dogs. Sometimes there would be chunks of rancid meat and other times flitches of bacon with a tangy taste due to insufficient salting. Canon Coodle, the parish priest, had roundly condemned these sacrilegious practices on many occasions but the grave-yard was convenient and there was little or no likelihood that the dumpers would be identified.

The Alsatians were near to starving when they entered the grave-yard. They lifted their heads high and sniffed the cold air when strange sounds drifted towards them from the far corner. Excitedly they bounded in that direction. They were at first mystified when they beheld the strange creature on all fours. Beyond doubt it was of the human species but on all fours it was fair game. After the first onslaught the savage canines became hysterical. The blood of the victim indicated more substantial fare to come. Frenziedly they dragged the screaming Sam into an area overgrown with white-thorn.

It was some days before a passing mourner, on his way to the isolated grave of a deceased relative, discovered the remains. He alerted Sergeant Ruttle who took charge of the investigation. An inquest was set in motion and under cross-examination the sergeant informed the jury that when he arrived at the scene he found that the body had been mutilated by animals which had since been destroyed. Some of Sam's ribs had been gnawed away and much of the flesh had been removed from the upper part of the torso. Pressed by the coroner Sergeant Ruttle revealed that rodents had consumed some of the victim's flesh.

Sam's wife Moya and their seven children flew home for the funeral. They never saw his remains.

Once the coffin was closed it would never be opened again. Neither would Sam's family ever be seen again in their native place but first they would wake their father as a father had never been waked before.

The little house was crammed for the occasion. Although the wake had a sluggish start it turned in the end into the most enjoyable extravaganza in the long history of parish obsequies. The paid mourners and the ordinary mourners were hard put to find a good word for Sam. Not one could show a tear and remember that between them in their lifetime they had shed enough tears to float the *Titanic*. Drink and goodwill circulated freely but there were no kind words. It was left to Fionnuala, the family's youngest member to set the eulogistic trend for the evening.

'God be good to my poor father,' she opened.

'Amen! Amen!' responded all present.

'We all know he blackened my eyes,' Fionnuala went on, 'and we all know he pulled out my hair. We know too he thumped me for no reason. He walloped me when I didn't deserve it. He growled at me and he howled at me and he scowled at me but he never bit me.'

'Amen! Amen!' sang the mourners.

Frank, the oldest son spoke next.

'He broke my two legs once,' Frank recalled.

'He fell on top of me from a ladder when he was drunk but he never complained.'

'Amen! Amen!' sang the mourners.

Entering into the spirit of the thing Moya spoke next. Her voice was broken but she managed somehow to hold it together so it wouldn't fall apart. 'God

grant that poor man a silver bed in heaven!' she cried
out fervently, 'for he had no bed of roses down here.
He suffered from a life-long thirst you wouldn't raise
in the hobs of hell but he never complained. He just
drank and drank and drank until that thirst was cured.
There was never a man like him.'

'There was never a man like him,' everybody
chorused.

'I recall well the time Frank broke his legs,' Sergeant Ruttle remembered in a fractured tone. 'Sam
Toper never reported it to me and he never reported
it to any other civic guard. He just put up with it because he was that kind of a man.'

'Amen! Amen!' came the assenting voices.

'And he never reported it to me either,' Dr Matt
Coumer recalled. 'He took it on the chin like the proud
father he was. We coffined a man today who will go
down in history.'

'Down in history!' the mourners echoed to a
man.

The wake was now buzzing. Drink in all its forms
flowed freely and no man or woman went hungry on
that memorable night. Holding Moya's hand in one
of his and his wife's Blossom O'Moone's in the other
Mental Nossery rose unsteadily to his feet. His voice
was hoarse with emotion when he addressed the mourners. He nodded his head in the direction of the coffin
and spoke: 'This was the noblest Toper of them all,'
he cried. 'I knew his brothers Jack and Mick and he'd
drink the two of them under the table. And is it not he
who is responsible for this banquet here tonight? There
would be no wake without him. This surely is the

greatest wake of all and I swear to this by the six breast nipples of the three musketeers. I say to you once and I'll say no more. I say to you that there was only one Sam Toper and no more.'

'Amen, amen!' sang Moya and her sons and daughters.

'Amen, amen,' sang Mental Nossery and his wife Blossom.

'Amen, amen!' sang out the great assembly of mourners while in the full-moon sky abroad in the night a lone star with a lengthening tail of silver whirred across the winking heavens to prove without doubt that another soul had arrived at the gates of heaven.

THE SEVEN YEAR TRANCE

This is the story of the strange disappearance of Hiccups O'Reilly. He did not disappear forever, only for seven years. 'They felt like a day,' he told his wife when he came home.

He was missing from Christmas Eve 1959 to Christmas Eve 1966 which was the very same day that Canon Cornelius Coodle landed the record-breaking thirty-four pound cock salmon in Pudley's Pool near the big bridge.

Hiccups' wife Delia did not believe him when he told her that he vanished while chasing a hare. He had been wearing a waist-coat made from the skin of his favourite greyhound bitch when he rose the hare in question on the slopes of Crabapple Hill overlooking the town. Hiccups was not called Hiccups because he was given to hiccupping. He was so called because he looked like a hiccup. Personally I do not know what a hiccup looks like. It's my guess, however, that it doesn't look good, that you wouldn't hang it on a wall for instance or you wouldn't give it to your children to play with.

Delia Hiccups' brothers, three in number, were built like tanks and made similar noises. Not once had they been seen to smile or laugh and whatever about Hiccups story of disappearing while chasing a hare the whole town and countryside would be on one word that the surest known way to disappear was to be in receipt of a mature, well-timed upper-cut from any single one of the six overgrown fists of the three aforementioned brothers, Mick, Dick and Slick.

Since Hiccups had already disappeared once he felt it would not be in his best interests to disappear twice so he stuck grimly to his story no matter the degree of incredulity it induced in his wife or her brothers Mick, Dick and Slick McCraw. Some believed his story, others did not. They said that Hiccups was a professional liar and that it was just the sort of tale they would expect from him. His friends and neighbours believed him or at least they said they did.

The story really began when Hiccups was presented with a beautiful greyhound bitch as a Christmas present by his uncle Ned. She was fawn in colour, moved like lightning, swerved like a footballer and could not resist the sight of a hare. The name they gave her was Flash. On her first outing she won the Trallock Bitch Sweep Stake which qualified her for a trip to the track in Limerick city for the final of another important stake. She won it easily and went on to win ten more big races before she was retired for breeding purposes. Alas she was never to breed because of an injury. She died soon after and so overcome with grief was Hiccups that he made a waist-coat out of her skin which he wore till the day he died. In fact, his enemies would say that it was the very same waist-coat he was seen wearing when he left Trallock railway station on that fateful Christmas Eve morning when he disappeared for seven years. His female companion was also wearing something, a perfectly-fitting blonde wig which ran down to the small of her back. Nobody knew who she was, that's if she ever existed but Hiccups' enemies insisted she was a voluptuous dame with false eyelashes and a well-developed bosom. Hiccups' friends would point out afterwards that there was no female missing from the parish or its surrounds so that the female seen with Hiccups – if seen – was no more than a casual acquaintance in whose vicinity he chanced to be prior to his departure.

I should have explained earlier that Hiccups was not warmly received by his wife after his long absence. In fact she locked him out and but for the intervention of Sergeant Ruttle and Canon Coodle he might never have seen the insides of his house again.

A week after his return his three brothers-in-law arrived at the house and demanded an explanation. They sat around the kitchen table and insisted that Hiccups join them. Hiccups knew that if his story was not accepted he would be beaten senseless so he wisely suggested to his would-be executioners that perhaps a sojourn in a nearby public house, such as Crutleys, might be more conducive to storytelling. The suggestion drew neither a hum nor a haw from Mick, Dick and Slick. When Hiccups intimated that he would be paying for all the drink consumed the brothers-in-law consulted with each other and with their sister who was not averse to a dollop of gin on occasion and they agreed that a public house might be a better proposition. The five proceeded to Crutleys at nine o'clock and found a particularly pleasant and secluded corner of the bar for the forthcoming revelations.

According to Hiccups he set out on the morning of Christmas Eve for open country, the morning it was alleged he left Trallock railway station with the wigged woman seven years before. He brought with him an elderly greyhound bitch for company and also in the half hope that they might rise a hare. He made his way to the slopes of Crabapple Hill and arrived there at noon. The day in question he reminded his brothers-in-law and their sister was a fine one with a wide blue sky and no sign of rain or storm, just a mild frost which saw their breaths, his and the dog's, rise in foggy plumes into the clear air where lark and linnet sang loud and high in praise of the weather. At this juncture Hiccups caught Fred Crutley's eye and signalled a refill.

While Fred did the needful the party spoke of the quality of local potatoes, coming down strongly in favour of Kerr's Pinks. They spoke of the spiralling price of beef and butter and of many other topics which affected their lives. They accepted the drinks gravely and without thanks and when they had the table to themselves they looked at their storyteller and waited for the resumption of his tale. Hiccups cleared his throat and licked his lips.

'Where was I?' he asked

'There was linnets singing,' his wife said.

'And larks,' the oldest of the brothers Mick reminded her gruffly.

'There were larks of course,' she agreed in the most conciliatory of tones.

'Correct on all counts,' Hiccups announced happily. 'I will never forget that day,' he went on, 'and not just because it was such a fine Christmas Eve but because of what befell me for I swear that there was magic involved. Didn't the hairs all of a sudden stand up on the top of my head the very same as darning

144

needles and didn't they tingle with music in the weak breeze that was just beginning to rise. After a while the bristles softened a little and were like what you would see on a coarse brush. The wind freshened all the while and sang in the heather.'

According to Hiccups the elderly bitch in his company suddenly sat down and refused to budge. He coaxed her but she whined and pined and whimpered which was most unusual because up until that time she was a brave and a game bitch without fear. The bitch then began to howl in a louder tone and the whole area at the western slope of Crabapple Hill brightened as though highlighted by spot-lights. It was then that the bitch rose unsteadily to her feet, raised her front paws aloft in the direction of her master indicating that he should quit the scene if he knew what was good for him. He endeavoured to mollify her a second time but all she did was drop her paws and turn her back on him after which she galloped off yelping, down Crabapple Hill at breakneck speed. She was not seen again for a very long time.

By now Hiccups was becoming a trifle apprehensive and when he heard the faint music of fairy pipes in the breeze he was between two minds whether he would stay on the hill or make for low ground. Ever a curious chap and coming from a long line of courageous sportsmen he proceeded to the very top of the hill where the sun shone as if it was the very height of June instead of Christmas Eve. Then for the first time he felt his waist-coat tensing and pulsating as though it was a living creature. There was silence now all over and then came a faint female voice, the most melodious and haunting ever heard by Hiccups.

'It wasn't the banshee,' he explained to his listeners, 'and it wasn't the sheegwee and it wasn't a lorgadán and it wasn't the man in the moon. I have heard in my time,' Hiccups continued, 'female singers from every part of the globe, sopranos, mezzo-sopranos and contraltos but none to match the bewitching tone that seemed to emerge from the very heart of the hill.' According to Hiccups he very nearly swooned and would have, he was sure, had it not been for the exceedingly fresh breeze, not a gale mark you, nor a wind but a refreshing breeze which filled him with extraordinary vitality. The strains of incredibly beautiful pipe music was now pouring forth from every crack, every cave, every hole and every cicatrice, every hollow and every dip on the vast hillside. All the while the fairy voice sang its haunting tunes. They tugged at the heartstrings until it seemed they must wilt and wither. They filled the mind with unworldly thoughts and the feet with a mad desire to leap and fly and dance. Even the heather at his feet seemed to be tugging at its roots such was its desire for escape into the skies where it would be free. Then, without warning of any kind, there was no sound save the fairy voice which now circled around his head and finally around the waist-coat fashioned from the skin of his favourite bitch of all time, the one and only Flash, Flash of the lightning turns and the speed of the fastest gale, Flash that had never been bested by a hare. Now the voice was calling a name.

At this exact stage when the tale was at its most gripping Hiccups caught the very watchful eye of

Fred Crutley – Fred who was never still, who never rested, who never seemed to take a break, who like the great barman that he was always hovered and never once intruded.

'Same again Fred!' Hiccups informed him.

During this interlude there was no small talk. His listeners including his wife were caught up in the story. The four came originally from a household in the far-off hills where there was more thought of a man who could tell a ghost story than there was of any professional man or any craftsman or any musician. Their faces were hungry for more for there was also an innocence underneath all the toughness and churlishness and the lack of good manners and it was on this basic innocence that Hiccups was depending for his physical welfare. While the innocence rose above the lesser traits and dominated their out-look and thinking he was safe. When the drink was served Fred moved out of ear-shot and swept the bar with his wary eye lest some unfortunate be denied his basic right to intoxicating liquor.

'Now!' said Hiccups, 'where was I?'

'They was calling Flash,' his wife informed him.

'They were not!' Hiccups was emphatic.

'Well,' said his wife, 'if they was not they was very near to calling her.'

'Don't argue woman!' Dick the second of the brothers cautioned her.

'Don't argue woman!' echoed Slick the youngest of the brothers.

They lifted their glasses and swallowed heartily. Then they directed their baleful eyes at their storyteller.

'This voice which was circling all around,' Hiccups resumed, 'was calling the name of my late greyhound bitch, my beloved Flash whose waist-coat I wear around my heart. "Flash, Flash, Flash", the voice called and I could feel the waist-coat trying to free itself off my body. "Flash, Flash, Flash!" it called again as the waist-coat struggled in vain to free itself.'

Then according to Hiccups the fairy voice materialised into a white hare. The hare hopped to and fro and danced provocatively in front of Hiccups and his darling waist-coat which was now trying to rip its buttons so that it could take off after the white hare. Failing to do so, the waist-coat took off anyway with Hiccups wrapped inside and with no say over his movements. He was obliged to follow the hare and his inadequate legs were doomed to chase wherever the hare decided to run. It ran, first of all, slowly up the hill as though it was giving the waist-coat a chance to catch up. It dawdled insolently as the waist-coat with Hiccups wrapped firmly inside tried to make up ground. All to no avail. The white hare, known far and wide as the fairy hare, lived in the depths of the hill, far, far underground, far from the sounds and sights of mixed-up humans. The hare now sat on its hind legs and started to call the waist-coat as though she was calling a cat.

'Peesh, peesh, Peesh, peesh,' she called.

Now nothing so infuriates a greyhound as comparison with a cat and Flash the greyhound bitch was no different. The waist-coat with Hiccups inside bounded up the hill and quickly gained on its tormentor.

The hare was lucky to escape as Hiccups legs worked overtime. As he tried to slow down Hiccups made the fatal mistake of digging in his heels. He turned several somersaults before coming to a halt. When he recovered and drew breath he saw the white hare sitting on a clump of heather far below him. He took off at once unable to restrain the waist-coat which was now at the height of its form and bent on nothing else but the tearing of the hare to shreds. As Hiccups bore down upon the hare the creature suddenly turned and went uphill again. Hiccups followed with no say over his movements. The waist-coat strained with all its might and its jaded owner had no choice but to follow. The hare took off in another direction when Hiccups drew near. The creature ran abreast of the hill along a lengthy level course. Now the hunt was on in real earnest.

The waist-coat started to bark as it neared its quarry. Hiccups found his own jaws directing themselves downwards, snapping and chopping and slobbering. His teeth almost seized upon the backbone of his would-be victim but all he got was a mouthful of white hair. The hare changed its course once more and now decided upon a rapid downhill run, avoiding nothing on its path, neither briar, nor nettle nor furze nor stream nor hole so that Hiccups was covered with scratches and blood and mud and drowned to the skin when the hare decided to stop for a breather half-way down the hill.

The waist-coat decided otherwise so that Hiccups found himself heading for a deep, soggy bog-hole at the bottom of the hill. In vain did he try to brake but the impetus was unstoppable. He roared at the top of his voice. He screamed in terror and cried out for the help as the moon started to rise over the top of the hill. Nobody answered his call. There was pipe music in plenty still coming from all sides and there was a great wailing and a great pillallooing coming from everywhere at once. Hiccups braced himself as the bog-hole drew near. He undertook a mighty leap in the hope that he might clear the obstacle and land at the other side. He landed, alas, right in the middle of the bog-hole with an almighty splash which sent frogs and newts and beetles scurrying for cover. So too did nesting wild ducks take off into the moon-lit skies as did freshly awakened larks, while stoats and rabbits and rooting badgers fled for their very lives. When Hiccups sank he was convinced he would never surface again but he reckoned without the waist-coat.

At this stage Hiccups beckoned to Fred who was now drinking a pint of stout in the company of Dr Matt Coumer, a routine to which he was addicted every single night of the week.

'Same again Fred!' Hiccups called as he examined the faces of his listeners.

They were enraptured not having heard a decent ghost story since their childhood. For the first time since his return Hiccups noticed a smile on his wife's face. It was a smile of sheer delight and it was directed towards her errant husband. The smile said that she was still mindful of his amorous skills and would not be averse to an embrace or even a kiss or even a hug or even a squeeze of longer duration culminating in a major make-up. She was still a fine looking woman and he often wondered why he had stayed away seven years. The answer came to him at once. Too many black eyes from the brothers as a result of her infernal complaining about him. If her smile was anything to go by she would desist from such reckless behaviour from now on.

When the drinks were delivered he found his hand being shaken by Matt Coumer who congratulated him on his safe return. There were others too who came forward and patted his back and spoke about the sad effect his absence had caused in all quarters.

'I hope you won't be as long away the next time you go,' said an innocent who had just entered. He retreated quickly due to the ferocity of the snarls and growls escaping from the porter-stained mouths of Mick, Dick and Slick. When all the well-wishers had retreated the storyteller and his listeners made themselves comfortable. They quaffed from their fresh drinks and gave the nod to Hiccups indicating that he was to proceed with his tale.

'Where was I?' he asked as he scratched his head.

'You was in the middle of getting drowned,' his wife reminded him.

'And were you drowned?' asked the three brothers in unison.

Hiccups did not answer at once. The wrinkles furrowed his forehead as he tried to accurately record the occasion.

'Ah yes!' he said to himself, happy that he remembered where he had left off.

'There I was at the bottom of forty fathoms of

bog-water, not able to swim, not able to see an inch, my lungs bursting for air when the waist-coat somehow inflated itself and brought me to the surface of the bog-hole.'

Apparently when Hiccups surfaced he found his hands paddling towards shore. The night was now master of the scene and the full moon played its role in lighting the hill and bog-lands. The stars twinkled over-head and it was at this stage that Hiccups found himself shivering with the cold. What with his wet clothes and the frost all around he concluded that pneumonia was inevitable.

'We have no time for that now,' the waist-coat seemed to say as it tensed and shook the water off before restarting the chase. Off they went, all three, at a frenetic gallop, the hare ahead by a yard or two all the time and Hiccups in hot pursuit with beads of sweat slowly replacing the beads of water on his brow. He began to huff and to puff and to fall and rise and roll over and tumble like an acrobat so fierce was the determination of the waist-coat at whose mercy he found himself.

Now came a furrowed field which they traversed at phenomenal speed. Now came a river which they leaped as though it were a rill. Now came a gate, over which they jumped as though they were steeplechasers. Now came a hollow, deceitful and deep. They descended like steeple-jacks and when they hit the ground they sped over a mushy swamp till they were fit to collapse with exhaustion.

Then of a sudden the white hare stopped without warning of any kind. The waist-coat stopped as well. She was enjoying the hunt too much to move in for the kill at that stage but the white hare seemed genuinely spun out. Feeble, heart-rending cries, almost human in their intensity, escaped her sagging mouth. Waist-coat and man looked on in amazement as the hare began to call a name. The place where the hare had stopped was rich in the most luxurious, multi-coloured growth, heavily-scented and of druggish potency so that waist-coat and wearer were very nearly overcome.

The name that the hare was calling was that of the queen of the local fairies Been-been of Coolnaleen. A long tongue of fire arose from the over-grown spot and a cave opening was revealed. The fire gave off no heat, merely a sleep-inducing warmth and an incense-like odour. Then bells began to tinkle all over the hill behind them, wraith-like under the moon's pale glow. It was an enchanting time if ever there was an enchanting time. As the white hare seemed to fall into a deep trance the waist-coat came to life and would have moved in for the kill had not a tall stately female of indeterminate age but of blinding beauty and disarming manner appeared near the very spot where the white hare lay. Weak as the creature was the whispered name of Been-been of Coolnaleen still carried from its lips.

The freshly arrived fairy, for fairy no doubt she was, placed a finger on her lips intimating to man and waist-coat that they must preserve the silence which now dominated the land. She withdrew from her garments a satchel woven from golden threads and the like of which Hiccups had never seen in all his travels. Even the waist-coat was stilled as the glow from the golden satchel cast its mellow light on the sleeping hare. She stroked the creature gently behind the ears until it began to purr like a kitten. Then she placed it in the satchel and cautioned Hiccups and his waist-coat.

'Nevermore will ye hunt on Crabapple Hill,' she told them. Her tones were far from being stern but there was a finality to them that made the hair stand on the head of Hiccups.

'The hare ye have chased,' she told them, 'is really a princess who was deprived of her human form by an evil witch who reigned on the hill until she was blasted by thunder and lightning and destroyed for ever more. The princess will regain her human form when the wild geese return to the flat lands of Cool-naleen and that should be very soon since they have been sighted close by for some time and it would not be any great wonder were they to appear next year or the year after.'

So saying she commanded a circle of fire to surround her as she disappeared into the hill-side. When she was gone there was no sign that the place had been visited by flame or by a queen from the other world or that a brave white hare had vexed a human and his hound that very day. As soon as she was gone the dawn, pale as death, came slowly to life and tinged the eastern sky with a multiplicity of delicate pastels. Hiccups fell to the ground and remembered not a single thing, and he gave his word on this, until he woke up in the middle of a fairy rath seven years later.

'Fred!' he called, 'be bringing us another round

like a good man.'

Fred landed shortly thereafter and placed the drinks on the table. Then he withdrew with a trayful of empty glasses and the price of the drinks. They quaffed from their glasses and toasted the courage and endurance of the white hare.

'Now!' said Hiccups, 'where was I?'

'You was after waking up in the middle of a fairy rath,' his wife told him, 'although 'tis a mystery to me how you stayed alive for seven years.'

'I was in a trance woman,' he explained.

'What do you think boys?' Mick asked Dick and Slick.

'I'll say nothing against fairies,' said Dick, 'although this man has the face of a born liar and I'll say that our brother-in-law wouldn't know the truth from a rumble in his belly.'

'As for me,' said Mick, 'I'll say nothing until we drink more for the way I judges is to judge when I'm sober and then when I'm drunk. I've already judged sober and it will take five or six more drinks before I'm drunk. I will say his tale was uncommon enough and worth hearing out but I'll have to wait till I'm soused.'

After that the drink flowed freely but never once did Mick or Dick or Slick test the material of their trousers' pockets so that the monies therein, if monies there were, were in no danger of being jingled or removed.

As soon as Mick had consumed the six extra pints he belched like a fog-horn and announced that he was about to pronounce judgement. 'I found the defendant guilty as hell for the first part of his story while I was sober and for the second part of his story while I was drunk I find him not guilty which is a blessing to our sister for she went very close to being a widow.'

'And the verdict?' his sister asked.

'The verdict is that he tells us a story once a week from this day forth in this very pub for the remainder of his natural life. Otherwise all charges against him are dismissed and he may go home with his wife to have and to hold from this day forth, wet or dry, windy or still.'

Hiccups wife threw her arms around him and thanked her brother Mick and the good God too. When Dick and Slick started to crónán and grumble they were silenced by Mick.

'We must forgive,' he said, 'especially since the twelve days of Christmas are not yet over. A ram has returned to the fold and for this we should be truly thankful.'

AWLINGAL PRINCESS OF
CUNNACKEENAMADRA

'Do you know what they remind me of?' Sergeant Bill Ruttle addressed his companion, Garda Sam Ruane, in low tones. The sergeant was referring to the brothers Mick, Dick and Slick McCraw who sat at a nearby table with their sister Delia and her husband Hiccups O'Reilly.

'What do they remind you of boss?' Sam asked out of the side of his mouth so that nobody would hear save the party for whom the question was intended.

'They remind me,' replied Bill, 'of three starving mongrels waiting for their scraps.'

Sam laughed loud and long, not out of loyalty to his sergeant but because he found the sergeant's comments in nine cases out of ten well worth laughing at. As Sam's guffaws subsided Fred Crutley approached the brothers' table with a tray upon which sat four pints of stout for the men folk and a gin for Hiccups' wife Delia.

As always the drink was paid for by Hiccups who was fulfilling the conditions laid down by the brothers on the very same night of the previous year which was the night before New Year's Eve. The conditions were that Hiccups would purchase all the intoxicating liquor that might be required to make the night a tolerable one and that he and his wife would meet with her three brothers once a week over their lifetime for no other purpose than the telling of stories especially those relating to the time Hiccups spent on Crabapple Hill while under a so-called trance.

'To date,' Bill confided to his friend, 'he has told fifty-one stories and it is my understanding that his three brothers-in-law are not at all pleased with the contents. On that first occasion this night last year he told a colourful and compelling tale and was acquitted of infidelity, absence without leave and what have you. Since that time,' Bill continued in a sad vein, 'the quality of the stories has deteriorated and the brothers have come to the conclusion that his version of events on Crabapple Hill is nothing but a collection of outrageous lies. They will surely kill or maim him unless he pulls one out of the hat tonight.'

'Well he won't be killed or maimed while we're here,' Sam assured his superior.

'Agreed, but the problem my dear Sam is that we won't be around all the time and our beloved superintendent is of the belief that placing a bodyguard on Hiccups would be a waste of time and money. He is convinced that the very most that can happen to Hiccups is maybe a fractured jaw or a few kicks on the rump or a black eye.'

'How does he know what will happen,' Sam asked, 'can he see into the future?'

'Exactly my friend,' Bill was serious now. 'As I see it those McCraw boys are capable of anything, maybe not outright murder but how many times have we seen bad beatings turn into killings! We'll play it by ear Sam and see what happens.'

'Maybe he'll come up with a masterpiece tonight,' Sam suggested.

'Don't bank on it my friend,' Bill's voice was filled with foreboding.

At Hiccups table there was an air of unease. The brothers Mick, Dick and Slick were jumpy to say the least. Their brother-in-law Hiccups was desperate. If his performance on this occasion was a flop like all the others in recent weeks the jig was up and it could well be the end of him.

Hiccups was a wealthy man, having inherited several substantial fortunes from uncles and aunts in America. If anything happened to him the money would go to his wife which was as good as saying that it would go to her brothers. Hiccups' wife Delia sat apprehensively by her husband. In the intervening year they had grown closer. She had forgiven him the long absence although she did not believe a single word about his ghostly sojourn on Crabapple Hill. She had to concede however that he had been a perfect husband since his return. He had showered her with presents. She had her own account in the bank and her weekly allowance was more than adequate. He was a loving and caring husband but she suspected that he had also been loving and caring with many other women. When Delia first found out about his philandering a few years into their marriage she had carried her troubles to her late mother who consoled her at the time by informing her that all men were the same in this particular respect, that it was the way they were made and if they did not behave thus there was something seriously wrong with them.

The couple were not blessed with children but Hiccups had promised her faithfully that if he did not raise a flag before the end of the springtime he would consider adopting a child. This had pleased Delia no end but it had not pleased Mick, Dick and Slick who felt that they had special claims to Hiccups' considerable wealth. Hiccups traded in horses and cattle when he was not at race meetings or football matches. Very often he took Delia with him but of late she had expressed a fancy for housekeeping and intimated gently to her sports loving husband that she was readying the house for a very special visitor.

Hiccups, against his will, was obliged to employ his brothers-in-law in a part-time capacity as cattle drovers and horse breakers on his large farm but so long as they did not intrude too much on his private life he suffered in silence. Now they were becoming out of hand but he reckoned that the arrival of his adopted son would change all that. The brothers would know exactly where they stood when his son and heir took up residence.

Just before Hiccups was about to commence his fifty-second instalment of the Crabapple saga his friend and sometime confidant Mental Nossery the poet arrived at Crutleys with his wife Blossom. The pair nodded civilly at the occupants of Hiccups' table and sat on a stool within a few feet of their friend. With snorts, scowls and other hostile emissions the Mc-Craw brothers thumped their table and let it be known that they would prefer if the newly arrived couple sat elsewhere. The Nosserys ignored the brothers and ordered a drink from a passing barmaid. The pub was soon filled to capacity. The spirit of Christmas was still abroad and there were many seasonal holidaymakers on the premises.

When Mick thrust his empty glass under his brother-in-law's nose Hiccups was on his feet instantly and managed to attract the attention of one of the two circulating barmaids on duty. When the drinks were served Hiccups cleared his throat and started in a tone audible only to the occupants of his own table and possibly in a garbled manner to a limited few who sat close by. 'The last creature I saw when I walked down the slopes of Crabapple Hill a year ago this Christmas was the queen of the fairies, the one and only Been-been of Coolnaleen. She barred my way and told me I was never to set foot on the hill again. I promised that I would do her bidding and to this day the heather up there, if it could talk, would tell you that Hiccups O'Reilly never sets foot there. She stood there for a while and passed her hand over me, not touching me but so near to my body that my flesh tingled and the hair stood on my head with each single rib extending itself and curling itself till it seemed that a thousand tiny antlers occupied my crown. It seemed to me too at the time that she was removing the spell that had been cast upon me at the beginning of my seven-year disappearance.'

When Hiccups paused to rejuvenate himself with a substantial swallow from his brimming pint the others did likewise. Hiccups took advantage of the lull to point a finger at Mick, the oldest and most superstitious of the three brothers.

'Beware,' said Hiccups in chilling tones, 'that you tread not on that part of the hill where I was waylaid by Been-been of Coolnaleen.'

'And why shouldn't I?' Mick asked as though he cared not in the least about fairies, be they queens or commoners.

'I'll tell you why you should care my good man,' said Hiccups in hollow tones. Hiccups went on to explain that Been-been, when she had fully removed the spell, placed her cold hands on his shoulders and looked with her flashing orbs into his own dazzled eyes. She then told him not to tell anything of what befell him unless his life depended on it.

'She told me that those who questioned my version would come to bad ends.'

When asked by a fearful Mick what sort of bad end Hiccups told him that according to Been-been the heads of doubters would be cut of by freak accidents such as falling on scythes or upright saws or electric wires. Mick McCraw dreaded threats from the other world more than any threat in this. He vowed to himself he would remain silent for the rest of the episode.

'Who else besides all those other wretches you told us about did you meet while you was up there?' The question came from Slick who was already yawning at the slowness and drabness of the Crabapple saga.

Hiccups paused for a moment to swallow from his glass and permitted himself one of the few smiles of the night. 'I'm downright glad you asked that question,' he responded, 'for on my third day under the spell and under the hill, as it turned out, who did I meet but a vet. He was surely three hundred years old with hair down to his boots back and front and it woven into a three piece suit which fitted him like it was tailor-made. Wasn't he the very same veterinary surgeon who treated the cow that jumped over the moon when she landed back on *terra firma*. He was a fine decent man with a smell of whiskey off his breath all the time which he claimed was as good as any antiseptic when one was around animals.'

Hiccups swallowed from his glass and availed of the opportunity to see how his tale was going down. There seemed to be a positive revival of interest and he had been aware of several intakes of breath at the mention of the cow that jumped over the moon. The cow in question had intrigued the McCraw brothers for many a year. The remainder of the rhyme they felt was preposterous and should not be taken seriously.

For instance they had been training cattle dogs all their lives and they had never once seen a dog laugh not to mention little dogs or pups like the one that laughed in the rhyme. As for the dish running away with the spoon, well that was complete nonsense as was the idea of a cat playing the fiddle. The one part of the rhyme that made sense to the McCraws was the cow that jumped over the moon. The McCraws might not know their oats as their neighbours might say and they certainly would not know their cate-chism which their teachers would verify and they knew nothing at all about women as any self-respect-ing woman in the parish would contend without fear of contradiction. But there was one creature they knew better than any other authority in the entire region and that was the bovine quadruped known far and wide as the cow.

But what kind of cow was it that jumped over the moon! It could not have been a mature cow at the peak of her milking output. She would be carrying too much fat and too much milk. Neither could it have been an in-calf heifer. She would not have the strength to jump over a decent hedge if she was carrying a calf. They had always felt that the cow that jumped over the moon was a heifer and a young heifer at that. However they could not be certain, not until now at least. All their lives they had chased other people's heifers, contrary creatures capable of jumping Beecher's Brook if the notion caught them, capable of clearing dykes and drains, ditches and hedges, gates and stiles, shrubs and bushes no matter the height. The Mc-Craws firmly believed that a young heifer was the most contrary creature in the known world. They had grown old before their time on the trail of lost heifers and now at last there was the hope of confirmation that it was a heifer and not a cow that jumped over the moon. They resolved to find out in their own circuitous fashion.

'What sort of chap was he?' Slick asked.

'What sort of chap was who?' Hiccups returned.

'The vet you fool,' Slick banged the base of his empty glass on the table.

'He was a nice chap if you liked chaps that picked their noses all the time and if you liked chaps that would fall asleep if you asked him more than two questions in a row.'

'Was he good on cows and heifers?' from Mick.

'He was.'

'Would he tell the age of a heifer just by looking at her?' Dick enquired.

'He would, he would,' Hiccups replied as he wondered what the brothers were driving at.

'Had he a wife and children?' Delia asked inno-
cently.

'Shut up you fool,' her brother Mick shouted and
gesticulated as though he would strike her.

'All right,' Slick was continuing, 'was she light in
weight, the heifer?'

'Light enough,' Hiccups assured him.

'It wasn't a cow then that jumped over the moon
then was it but a heifer,' Slick suggested thrusting his
thumbs inside his galluses as if he was a barrister.

'It was a five year old cow,' Hiccups informed him.

'You're a liar sir,' Slick roared. It was the first time
that Slick had addressed Hiccups as sir. He hadn't yet
shed his barrister image.

All the brothers were shouting together now but
the essence of all the tumult was that it was not a cow
that jumped over the moon.

'How,' they asked 'could a five year old cow jump
over the moon?'

'There is no way a five year old could do it,' Mick
was insisting, 'and you're insulting my intelligence
by saying so whereas,' he went on, 'whereas, whereas
...' he repeated the word, never having used it before
and very much liking the sound of it. For Mick finding a new word was like an embattled soldier finding
a new and deadly weapon.

'Whereas,' Mick rose to his feet, 'it would be no
trouble to a two year old heifer to jump over the moon
especially if she was on the road to a fair in the early
morning and especially if she had never seen anything but hedges and grass before her outing. I've

seen heifers jump over low clouds when the mood caught them.'

'Me too,' said his brother Slick pounding the table, 'I seen a bony heifer one morning jump over myself and I'm six feet.'

Dick was next to enter the controversy. 'Anyone,' said Dick heatedly, 'what says it was a cow jumped over the moon should have his nose broken and maybe his jaw.'

'That settles that then,' Slick concluded. 'The court finds,' he announced as he placed an ashtray on his head, 'that it was no cow jumped over the moon but a heifer and he's a dead man that says otherwise.'

Hiccups felt that if he had known what his brothers-in-law were driving at he would have said that it was a heifer that jumped over the moon and not a cow. Under the glare of the inquisition however he had lost his composure.

'Now that I come to think of it,' put in a pale-faced Hiccups, 'I think the veterinary surgeon said that it was a heifer jumped over the moon and not a cow.'

'Too late to back-track,' Slick placed a beefy hand around the slender neck of his brother-in-law and held him like a vice.

'We've heard what you said. You said it was a five year old cow, not two, three or four but five. A cow is what you said you rotten liar what wouldn't know the word of truth from a sneeze.'

Mick was next to cast judgement. 'You're a re-gistered liar, a department liar, a perverted liar and if you lied in one thing then you lied in all things. You never spent seven years in a trance you sacrilegious belch. You spent seven years hooring and touring in England and France and maybe America and Australia too. You soon got tired of that peroxide blonde you took with you and you took up with others and left our poor sister in the lurch.'

'Well we're happy now,' Delia trembled as she said her piece.

'Let him go,' Mick instructed his brother Slick. 'My glass is empty and there's no way he can call for a drink while you have a hold of him like that.'

While the drinks were being delivered Sam Ruane addressed his sergeant in a whisper: 'I don't like it boss,' he said.

'Neither do I Sam,' said Bill, 'but I wouldn't worry too much. We'll bide our time and play the tune by ear when the last dance is called.'

'These birds have changed,' Mental Nossery whispered into his beautiful wife's ear after he had first nibbled its lobe. 'Ever since word went out that Hiccups and Delia were thinking of adopting a baby,' Mental continued, 'the brothers McCraw have assumed a different air of menace. If a new baby comes in, it means that they go out, and sooner or later. Hiccups life could be in danger.'

Blossom seized her husband's hand, her poet's hand. 'You mean that they might kill him!' she asked tremulously.

Mental whispered into his beloved's ear a second time but left the lobe alone. It was not an occasion for levity and Mental with his poet's insight sensed that there were dark clouds on the horizon.

'I'll tell you this and no more,' he told her, 'wherever there is disputed land you can't rule out a killing.'

'What can we do?' she asked fearfully.

'Worry not my pet, my peach,' Mental told her after the fashion of poets through the ages. 'Hiccups is not without friends as you shall see. He who rides the white steed of chivalry will carry the day and the sun will shine on a better world.'

'You're so brave my warrior poet,' Blossom whispered.

Blossom Nossery, formerly the lovely Blossom O'Moone, liked Hiccups. He never made passes, having too much regard for her husband Mental. Once he had given her his umbrella in a downpour and told her it was an honour. He had been corner forward on the cherished Ballybo team which won two titles in a row and most important of all he was godfather to her oldest son and his wife Delia was godmother. She watched him now as he looked with a mixture of terror and hope at her bardic warrior, her writer of epic poems, her shield and her champion, her sweetheart and her lover.

After Fred Crutley had deposited the fifth round of drinks on the table he was asked by Hiccups for the correct time.

'There is plenty of time my friend,' Fred informed him.

'Are you going some place?' Slick asked with thinly-veiled sarcasm.

Before Hiccups could answer Mick posed a second question: 'what are you hatching Hiccups? It isn't eggs and that's for sure and you are hatching for I seen that look on a goose many a time.'

'Maybe,' Dick broke out into a rare laugh, 'he's catching a train and don't want to be late!'

'Another blonde maybe!' Slick guffawed.

Hiccups was sorry for his wife. The embarrassment showed clearly on her face. He wished he could place his arms around and assure her that he would never again leave her but the brothers-in-law were demanding another round of drinks.

Most of the patrons had already left the bar. With New Year parties in the offing they wanted to be fresh for the festivities. One by one they drifted out into the night. A sickle moon hung limply overhead and a magnificent array of stars twinkled in the heavens.

Normally Fred would approach Hiccups' table on the stroke of midnight and remind the occupants that they could no longer stay. Tonight it was different. When Slick asked if there was any hope of another round of drinks Fred told him that there was every hope. The only reason that Slick had asked for drinks in the first place was because he thought he would be refused. He instructed Hiccups to pay up or else.

Those who remained on in the bar were strangely silent. Not even a whisper was to be heard. Mental and Blossom still remained as did Bill Ruttle and Sam Ruane; so too did the Badger Loran and his wife Nonie. Maimie Crutley had earlier joined her friends Badger and Nonie at a table near the main doorway. A few regulars sat discreetly out of range of the main table which was occupied by Hiccups and his tormentors. The only absentee of note was Dr Matt Coumer. Earlier in the evening he had been seen driving out of town at a pace far faster than usual.

'It couldn't have been a patient,' the observer said, 'because Matt would never drive like that on his way to see a patient. It must have been something really important.'

All of a sudden the lights were dimmed in the bar and the sound of eerie music drifted downwards from somewhere in the ceiling. It was undoubtedly the sound track from a horror movie.

'What's it from Sam?' Bill asked his colleague.

'It's from "Dracula's Daughter meets the Werewolf's Son",' Sam answered without a moment's hesitation.

'All knowledge is useful,' Bill pointed out as he lifted his glass and concentrated his vision on the main doorway.

Just then the bar lights were extinguished altogether and the pub's only spotlight shone on the doorway which seemed to hold so much interest for the sergeant. The music ceased and a roll of drums sharpened the interest of everybody present, most notably the three McCraw brothers. Cowards at heart they dreaded the darkness even when surrounded by other humans.

The roll of the drums intensified and there was the sound of a protracted scream from the doorway. The pub cat, a fat and less than frisky tabby, shrieked her way out of doors and was not seen for days. Silence again prevailed.

Nervously the McCraw brothers raised their glasses but lowered them untouched when a low and ghastly moan came from the direction of the doorway. Enter a dark stranger. He wore a black beard and moustache and was garbed like an Elizabethan gentleman. Slung over his shoulder was a large satchel woven from golden threads. When he laid it on the floor one couple could plainly hear the mewing and the bleating and the aforementioned moans coming from within.

Delia slipped silently from her chair on to the floor in a dead faint. Her exit from consciousness went unnoticed so absorbed was every watcher by the unbelievable goings-on at the doorway.

The table where the McCraw brothers sat began to shake as the trembling wretches transmitted their terror to the lifeless wooden surface where the glasses now tinkled and jumped and rolled over as though electrified. The brothers could have exited in a flash but so overcome were they by terror that their legs refused to move. On the other hand Hiccups was elated and quite carried away by recent events.

Hot on the heels of the Elizabethan satchel-carrier came a tall, stately if somewhat gaunt woman dressed completely in black with a ruff round her neck and a silver comb thrust deep into the bun of her tightly drawn hair.

'Is she ...' Mick McCraw asked in terror, his voice shaking, 'is she Been-been from Coolnaleen the queen of the Crabapple Hill fairies?'

'None other!' came the proud response from Hiccups.

'And is the creature in the satchel,' Mick asked, 'the same hare yourself and the waist-coat coursed that first time you climbed Crabapple Hill?'

'She is one and the same hare!'

Again there was pride in Hiccups voice.

'And, and, and,' Slick asked brokenly, 'will she be changed tonight into a princess.'

'Yes. Yes,' Hiccups answered impatiently.

'Hear ye! O hear ye!' came the awesome and ponderous voice of the Elizabethan satchel-carrier, 'Behold the transformed white hare of Crabapple Hill.'

The words had no sooner left his lips than the queen of the Crabapple fairies knelt on one knee and opened the golden satchel. Extending her hands she commanded the creature in the satchel to come forth. Forth she came, a dazzling and beautifully shaped young lady with a glittering diamond tiara on her brow and golden slippers on her shapely feet.

'Behold!' said the Elizabethan satchel-carrier, 'the Princess Awlingal, rightful sovereign of Cunnackeen-amadra and all parts west.'

The McCraws could not contain their shuddering and agitation. When Mick spoke his speech was slurred and broken.

Meanwhile Hiccups had noticed his wife's plight and placed her on a chair beside his own. He poured brandy into her mouth and she regained consciousness. They looked into each other's eyes and wondrous smiles appeared on their faces.

'What in God's name are you blabbering about man?' Hiccups with a newly discovered confidence asked his distraught brother-in-law.

Mick McCraw asked if the woman at the doorway was the same Been-been from Coolnaleen he had met on Crabapple Hill and if the transformed hare was really Awlingal the sovereign Princess of Cunnackeenamadra and all parts west.

'That's who she is for sure,' Hiccups answered still growing in confidence from watching the abject terror of his brothers-in-law.

'There is one sure way to find out,' Slick put in as he found his coherency returning to him.

'And what way would that be?' asked Dick who had been frothing at the mouth in fear a few short moments before.

'You remember,' Slick reminded his brothers, 'how Hiccups here told us he bit the back of the white hare as they coursed over Crabapple Hill and how he brought a clump of hair away with him. Now if that be so there surely has to be a mark on the back of the princess.'

As though their words had carried to all within the room the spotlight was turned off and the full bar lights turned on. Led by the Elizabethan satchel-carrier the queen of all the Crabapple Hill fairies and the Princess of Cunnackeenamadra and all parts west marched towards the table of the McCraws, the stout heels of their knee-length leather boots striking the timber floor in unison and bringing a sense of majesty to the occasion. The Elizabethan satchel-carrier raised a gloved hand imperiously and spoke in ringing tones: 'Hear ye! Oh hear ye!' He cast his stern countenance in the direction of Slick.

'Rise knaves!' he commanded at which the three brothers struggled terror-stricken to their feet and doffed their filthy caps in the direction of the royal pair.

'Now speak lest I draw my blade and disembowel the three of ye,' the Elizabethan satchel-carrier commanded. The cowardly trio at once began to blame each other and denied having any interest in seeking the hidden evidence which would prove forever that the Princess of Cunnackeenamadra was indeed the rightful sovereign of the territories attributed to her. Suddenly there was a flash of steel as the satchel-carrier withdrew his sword from his scabbard. He pointed the blade at the Adam's apple of Slick and informed him that he would cut his head off if he did not speak.

'All I want to know sir,' said the cringing Slick, 'is whether or not there is a mark on the back of this girl, a mark made by human teeth to be exact?'

'On thy knees thou most disrespectful of wretches where my hungry blade may relieve thee of thy head.'

'Nay, nay!' said the princess in voice most melodious and with that she raised her dress and revealed a scantily clad but shapely posterior without blemish of any kind. A gasp escaped the audience. It was not occasioned by the undeniable shapeliness of the royal rump but rather by the fact that there was a dark red disfiguration on the small of the back just over the the right cheek of Princess Awlingal's rear.

'What say you now sir?' asked the Elizabethan.

'I say was it caused by the teeth of a human?' Slick was surprised at his own audacity.

'If I may!' Sergeant Ruttle rose to his feet and handed his cap to Sam.

'My Lord!' he addressed himself to the Elizabethan who graciously acknowledged his presence with an economical but respectful curtsy.

'I am obliged to say at the outset,' Bill opened, 'that the mark on this most attractive area was not caused by human teeth, by teeth yes but not by teeth that grow in the mouth of a human. Rather was the mark made by these.' He extended his hand towards Hiccups who extracted his dentures from his mouth and handed them to the sergeant. Bill ordered all the interested parties to gather round the Princess of Cunnackeenamadra. He held Hiccups false teeth aloft and slowly lowering them placed them over the disfiguration at the top of the right buttock.

'Are they a fit?' Slick asked.

'They are,' said the sergeant triumphantly, 'a precise fit and that concludes the evidence My Lord.'

Bill and the Elizabethan exchanged the most civil of nods.

When it dawned fully on the McCraw brothers that their brother-in-law had proven connections with the underworld they pushed their chairs back from the table in order to put as much distance between themselves and the lorgadán as possible. They eyed their sister with suspicion and for the first time, began to perceive out of their fear and ignorance, underworld subtleties and fairy-like fragilities transforming her placid features. Slowly, noiselessly, stealthily they rose from their seats and stood momentarily transfixed. Then at a signal from the oldest brother Mick they ran from the bar, overturning chairs, tables and stools and beseeching the great God of their fathers to save them.

In Crutleys there was unconfined delight. The participants in the charade turned out to be members of the Trallock Amateur Drama Group with the following cast in order of appearance:

Elizabethan Satchel-carrier	Matt Coumer
Been-been Coolnaleen	Roseanna Ruane
Princess Awlingal	Bridget Ruane
Counsel	Bill Ruttle
Producer	Maggie Coumer
Lighting	Canon Coodle
Stage Manager	Dotie Tupper
Music	Tom Mackson
Costumes	Mickey Mokely
	Dotie Tupper
Front of House	Fred Crutley
Concept	Mental Nossery

In the years ahead the brothers gave Hiccups and Delia a wide berth and covered their faces with their hands when ever they met lest they make contact with the eyes of either and be consigned forever to supernatural botheration.

When the two adopted sons of Hiccups and Delia reached boyhood a reconciliation was effected and the McCraw brothers devoted their lives to their nephews' upbringing.

The Sacred Calf

If you were suddenly to leap from behind a furze bush, seize my throat in both hands and threaten me with strangulation if I didn't tell you the truth, I could hardly tell a lie could I!

If you were to ask me as your grip tightened which was the most memorable Christmas in the history of our parish I would say without hesitation that it was the Christmas of the sacred calf. You will no doubt have heard and read of sacred cows but I'll lay a fat goose to a starving sparrow that it's the first time you've come across a sacred calf; golden calves yes, castrated calves yes, fatted calves yes, but sacred calves no!

The calf in question was born on St Patrick's Day, a spindly, knock-kneed chap the image of his grandfather and this is where the catch comes in. The father, if you get my drift, was suspect or if you like he was rejected for procreational purposes by an inspector from the Department of Agriculture on the grounds that his shoulders were exaggerated and he was also, alas, possessed of a somewhat contracted rump, features indeed which were often highly prized in his human counterparts by certain females, at least in this parish or so it is claimed by those who should know. Although the sacred calf himself suffered from no such so-called defects he might nevertheless be branded as undesirable for breeding purposes.

The sacred calf's owner, one Jackeen Coyne, was undecided about the creature's future. 'I could,' he told his wife, 'deprive him of his population stick and turn him into a prime bullock in the course of time or I could hold on to him and let him take his chances with the inspectors from the department.'

'You could sell him in a few weeks for veal or you could hold on to him until Christmas when he'd be just right for baby beef. Baby beef is all the go now,' his wife reminded him, 'but by that time he might be shaping towards a passable bull so you wouldn't have anything to lose.'

Jackeen, like most of the farmers in the district, always paid heed to what his wife suggested. Wives had no vested interests like butchers or calf-jobbers. They listened to the agricultural programmes on the radio and had a fair idea of what was going on. So it was that Jackeen opted for baby beef.

It had all begun the previous summer when a scrub bull or a Walkeen Aisy as he would be known locally entered the scene or rather broke into the well-fenced acres of Jackeen. The owner of the marauding scrub was a happy-go-lucky sort, one Mickey Martin, who rarely mended his fences and might never have done so had not Jackeen threatened him with the law on numerous occasions. It was left to Jackeen to secure his heifers by constant fence-mending and extreme vigilance by himself and his wife all day and all night from early springtime onwards. Jackeen's pure-bred Friesian heifers, eight in number, were separated from the remainder of the mixed herd for breeding purposes and were truly the apples of their proprietor's eye. He walked among them morning and evening after the herd had been milked. He noted their sprightliness and playfulness and allowed that they were a prime lot well worth the time invested in them.

When the scrub bull could no longer contain himself he became increasingly agitated. Normally this agitation might not appear until the late autumn when he would have expended all his energies. This particular form of agitation, however, was different. It was, if you'll forgive the pun, born out of mounting frustration. He was a young bull and had already accounted for all of his master's cows and heifers.

Jackeen redoubled his labours at the fences and would look apprehensively through the well-stitched thorn hedge at the restless fornicator who rarely took his eyes off the forbidden fruit in the next field. Jackeen decided to change his charges to more distant pastures at the earliest opportunity. On the other hand Mickey Martin cared not a whit for the state of his fences or the sexual ardour of his scrub. When Jackeen spotted him one evening on his way to town he shouted after him that he should move the scrub to another field.

'You get your Friesians to stop teasing him,' Mickey called back before disappearing through a gap in another pasture. Meanwhile Jackeen fretted and fumed as he awaited the arrival of the department inseminator, an industrious young man already working round the clock in order to fulfil his many commissions. Jackeen's nights were sleepless. He would rise several times from his bed as would his wife. From their upstairs window their eyes swept the moon-lit fields but the bull was nowhere to be seen. Occasionally they would hear him bellow and there came a time when Jackeen would hear bellowing in his imagination until black rings began to appear under his eyes.

So jaded had he and his wife become from their sapping vigils that they went straight to bed after the evening milking and rarely visited the cavorting Friesians who taunted their mesmerised admirer with swishing tails and fancy steps. Then of a sudden when he could endure the anguish no longer the scrub found a gap in the hedge. It was only a small gap but by the time he had forced his way through it was considerably larger, certainly large enough for the pure-bred Friesians, no longer mindful of their vaunted pedigrees, to pay return visits to the paddock of their less exalted pursuer. In record time Mickey's tireless impregnator accommodated each and every one of the eight heifers. Amazingly he showed no loss of taspy after his endeavours but he did, according to a boastful Mickey, have a long and sound sleep for himself, in case he might be called into action again.

In the spring of the following year the cows calved. One of the five bull calves presented to the world by the pedigreed Friesians stood out above the others. Although spindly and knock-kneed at birth as we have said he assumed his true pose and carriage after a few days.

Eventually Christmas began to advertise its proximity. The streets of the nearby town took on a carnival atmosphere and indulgent parents made haste to book their personal Santa Clauses in advance of the great feast day. There was an air of excitement abroad and a heart-warming type of burgeoning goodwill which only Christmas can generate. Then came the great

Christmas cattle fair, an annual event which drew cattle of all ages and breeds from far and wide. The great square in the nearby town was the traditional venue and although the square boasted two churches, one Catholic and the other Protestant, it was conceded by reverent and irreverent alike that no other place had the capacity to accommodate the large numbers of livestock and their owners.

Jackeen and his wife Maryanne were plain to be seen. Maryanne's presence was imperative if the eight weanlings they offered for sale were to be prevented from straying. Jackeen and Maryanne carried light hazel sticks more for intimidation than physical punishment. Brandishing was sufficient, for the most part, although from time to time the more adventurous had to be rounded up and returned to the preserved area outside the main entrance to the Catholic church. It was here that all the generations of Coynes as far back as anybody could remember were known to have traditional standing rights for their stock. With Christmas only a week away, and money scarce or so the farmers maintained, the Coynes were anxious to dispose of their weanlings before the fair ended and darkness fell. Their Christmas shopping would follow.

They had arrived at their small domain outside the church at seven o'clock and, as the early morning hours lightened, the jobbers were afforded better conditions to inspect what was on offer. There had been several tentative approaches from first light. None was satisfactory although there was a farmland saying about an owner being better advised to accept the morning price. Jackeen, however, suspected that the adage was originally invented by the jobbers. It would be true to say that farmers always suspected jobbers in the first place and would bide their time until the market settled and the vendors had consulted each other about prices.

Maryanne was already well versed in such matters having been tuned in to the agricultural programmes on radio and television for weeks before. It was she who put an asking price on the eight weanlings consisting of five bull calves and three heifers. As expected the buyers wanted only the special bull calf who was a far more attractive specimen of his species than his brothers or sisters.

'Pity they hadn't the pure drop in them,' Jackeen declared angrily to his wife on more than one occasion when he went to count them. 'I promise you I wouldn't be selling but with their father a scrub what can I do?'

'We'll do fine,' Maryanne assured him. 'They're good-looking weanlings all. They'll make my price. You'll see now.'

Sure enough as the morning hastened towards noon the offers began to improve until Maryanne's reserve was nearly reached. The square, by this time, was chockablock with cattle young and old. Calves bawled for their milk and as the shouting of jobbers and cattle-tenders intermingled with the bawling and bellowing of hungry cattle there was a situation akin to pandemonium in the great square. Then and only then did Maryanne notice the absence of Blueboy, the pet name with which they had christened the cherished bull calf. They searched high and low but there was no trace of their pride and joy. Jackeen later admitted that he had been reluctant to offer him for sale in the first place. Opinions among local experts had been divided as to whether he would pass the bull test when his time came. Some voted nay and some voted yea. Between the jigs and the reels Jackeen decided to sell. He would reseed the Friesian heifers the following spring and he would make sure that the inseminator got to them before Mickey's scrub.

In desperation Jackeen engaged some local youngsters to search for the calf. All they brought back were conflicting reports. One had seen the weanling crossing the river and another had spotted him disappearing into a lane-way. When the lane-way was searched there was no trace of the missing calf.

It was then that Maryanne decided to invoke the aid of St Francis of Assisi. Rosary beads in hand she entered the adjacent church where she quickly located a plaster statue of the Franciscan founder, and head bent in supplication, she prayed for the recovery of the missing weanling. Normally she would spend an hour and sometimes longer on her knees but her husband would be waiting. As she was about to leave the church she was surprised to see a large crowd gathered in the vicinity of the crib. Some were tittering and smiling. Others wore serious expressions. Despite her hurry she allowed her natural curiosity to get the better of her. She forced her way through the gathering and wondered what the attraction might be. Another moving statue perhaps or maybe one of the plaster occupants of the crib was bleeding! She knelt at the crib railing and closed her eyes the better to concentrate on her prayers and also to convey the impression to the watchers all around that she had no interest in anything bar her own supplications.

After the third Hail Mary she opened her eyes and could scarcely believe what she saw before her. There lay Blueboy with a contented look on his face, his mouth stuffed with high grade straw. He had taken up his position between the life-sized cow and donkey where he knew he would be safe.

Earlier his nostrils had been assailed by the odour of freshly-disturbed straw. Compared to the graveolence all around him this was truly a heaven-sent fragrance which had to be investigated. He made his way into the church, empty save for the presence of a few elderly people who would hardly have noticed had a lion appeared in front of the main altar. Blueboy was reassured by the presence of the other animals and had no trouble in making his way into the crib where he attempted to satisfy his hunger. The first person to notice something out of the ordinary was an old man, a regular visitor to the crib from the moment the parish clerk had erected and populated it.

'I declare to God,' he said with a smile on his wrinkled face, 'if it isn't a sacred calf.' His words carried to the ears of two old ladies nearby who had waited all their lives for some manifestation of recognition from the spiritual world.

'A sacred calf.' They echoed the words with awe and reverence and when Maryanne blinked her eyes in disbelief as the old ladies whispered into her ear from either side of her she nodded good-humouredly. She hurried into the square to tell her husband the good news. He threw his arms around her in delight and lifted her high in the air. Did I say earlier on, that they were a young couple and very much in love! Maybe not. I should have and I'm sorry I didn't but it's out now and we'll all be the better for it.

Jackeen recovered his calf and brought him back into the fold.

'I say to you,' he said to his wife with a twinkle in his eye, 'that a calf which is lost and then found must be kept.'

So it was that Jackeen disposed of the remaining calves at a fair price and so too did he hand over the money to his wife for she would surely make better use of it than he. That night as they lay in bed they spoke of the day's events and recalled the recovery of the sacred calf with much laughter.

'We will never part with him,' Jackeen promised Maryanne, 'for as sure as that's a wind in the curtains it was a message from above we received this day.'

'St Francis had a hand in it,' Maryanne reminded him. 'We'll say a prayer to him now in thanksgiving.'

'He'll make a powerful bull,' Jackeen whispered when the prayer was finished.

Jackeen's prophesy came true. Two years later the sacred calf was presented for inspection at Abbeyfeale cattle fair. The inspector from the Department of Agriculture declared that in all his days he had never come across a more promising bull.

'His grandfather was a latchiko,' the inspector recalled meaning that the parent in question was sometimes remiss in his obligations towards consenting heifers and often turned his back on what more industrious bulls might regard as golden opportunities.

'His father now was a different kettle of fish,' the inspector went on, 'and could not be kept away from members of the bovine species regardless of age. Luckily for the future of the cow population of this country the bull I have just passed is the image of his father in this respect.'

Christmas came with some gentle flurries of snow and if the nights were cold itself Maryanne was able to announce to her doting husband that the cow population wasn't the only outfit that could expect an increase in the following year. On hearing the news Jackeen leaped from his bed and with a series of delighted whoops danced around the room until he was totally exhausted. In the years ahead the rescued bull would account for countless cows and heifers and like all great bulls he treated young and old with equal tenderness and affection so that he had many calls upon his extravagant nature. I might well have called this tale 'The Sacred Bull' but because of the season that's in it I think we should call it 'The Sacred Calf'.

Two Gentlemen of the Law

Forty years ago our public house was raided by two elderly members of the garda síochána, two gentlemen if ever there were gentlemen as you shall see if you proceed to the finish. For the benefit of those in other lands a member of the garda síochána is simply a member of the police force.

The exact time was the night before Christmas Eve and a stormy night it was with a stiff sleet-laden easterly gale confining many of the town's drinking fraternity to their homes. Not so the intrepid folk of the town's hinterland. They braved the elements and drank their fill. They would not drink again until St Stephen's night or the night of the wren as they called it.

The only creatures to be seen out of doors were tomcats for, as everybody knows, your common tom-cat cannot survive without regular sexual excursions into the night. I have lost count of the times I have encountered exhausted tomcats returning to their bases even on the sacred occasion of Christmas night. A creature with nine lives has surely nine sexual drives or so people say.

There were also two members of the garda abroad or so it was rumoured but it was believed that they were not engaged in public house duties. This could be deduced, by experienced observers, from their gait and miens and general attitude. They strolled round the streets rather than policed them so the proprietors of public houses could not be blamed if they presumed they were in for an easy ride on the occasion.

In our own premises there were a half-score of hardened public house denizens whose love of liquor far exceeded their fear of storms. It wasn't that they drank excessively. Rather did they lower a few pints to cure what ailed them and help them get over the sleeplessness which affects so may souls on stormy nights. They were called regulars and at that time every public house in the town had its quota. Uncharitable members of the community would accuse them of being drunkards and ne'er-do-wells but the more charitable would say that they were merely anxious for drink.

That time there were roughly seventy public houses in the town. Now there are only forty. You could say that time caught up with the vanished thirty. Let us proceed, however, with our tale of Christmas benignity and let it serve as a reminder that kindnesses are remembered when insults are forgotten – that charity and chivalry are cherished when boors and begrudgers are benighted.

In those days I had a man working for me on a part-time basis. When he finished milking his employer's cows he came to me to tap barrels, to box bottles and to keep an eye on the back door among other things. You might say that keeping an eye on the back door was his chief duty. It was an onerous chore calling for vast experience in the ways of the world. When the prescribed number of knocks were knuckled on the back door he would admit the knocker or knockers. The door was a stout one and no one could look out unless one knelt or lay down to look underneath. Neither could anybody see in and no self-respecting policeman would stoop to peep when, by merely announcing his presence, admission would be automatic by virtue of the authority invested in him by the state.

But, the dear reader will ask, suppose a guard knuckled the secret knock after hours what would be our man's reaction? There would be no reaction for the good reason that no self-respecting member of the garda síochána would stoop to such a ruse. All guards liked to knock imperiously on the door and intone the time-honoured caution: 'Guards on public house duty!'

How then would my doorman respond to this official knock? My man whose name was Jimmy Jay would first kneel and then rest his head sideways on the ground where he could look out under the door to make sure that it wasn't a local prankster assuming the role of guardian of the peace. If the knocker wore grey shoes or brown shoes, suede shoes or white shoes or wellingtons he was admitted by Jimmy Jay. Members of the garda síochána wore only black shoes or black boots while on duty. There was another, equally important, guideline in the identification process – guards on duty had no folds on their trousers. All punters, therefore, with folds on their trousers were seen to be above suspicion and were granted immediate entry. This, let me state at this important juncture, is how our story came about. Let me put it another way. If there were no folds no story would unfold and we would be without material for our yuletide tale.

I don't have to tell my readers that this is a true story. The men who were present in the public house that night will bear witness to its veracity.

Now let us adjourn to the outside world, to wit the windy streets of my native town where our limbs of the law were sauntering along the main streets and the little streets, the big square and the small square and the limited suburbs where nothing ever happened. Seemingly casual and somewhat lackadaisical on their patrol it has to be said that nothing could be further from the truth for the good reason that our pair of custodians missed little. Not a blind was drawn or raised nor a solitary curtain opened without their committing it to memory. The number of strangers were counted, their mannerisms and physical features noted with care and every shadow was pierced by the experienced eyes of our alert duo.

The names of our patrollers were Mike and Jerry. The pair rarely troubled the town's public houses except when called upon to do so by the proprietors of the public houses in question when the latter might become apprehensive in the face of blackguardism. Others who sometimes got in touch with the guards were mothers of large families whose husbands were recklessly squandering their wages on liquor and allowing their children to starve. Other informants might be the occasional publican who would be acting out of jealousy or just plain, ordinary malice. In such instances the members of the force had no option but to investigate and issue summonses where necessary. Rarely did they prosecute the wretch who so profligately spent his wages. Instead they quite rightly prosecuted the publican and administered several well-aimed kicks to the posteriors of the aforementioned wretches. These kicks worked wonders but today it is against the law.

Anyway our jolly policemen, and jolly they were unless provoked, encountered a drunken wretch on the street. He claimed that he had been refused drink here on these very premises because of his politics. The truth is that he was refused drink because he was abusing his wife and family when under the influence. The limbs of the law, however, had no choice but to investigate the goings-on behind our closed doors. They would do so without fear or favour. They had spent the greater part of the day papering and painting some rooms in Mike's house. Mike was expecting American visitors in the spring, cousins of his wife, and who better to help him than his colleague and long-term friend.

The pair proceeded to our back door where Jimmy Jay sat in an out-house awaiting knockers. Jimmy was slightly deaf. He heard the guard's knock all right but he didn't hear them announce themselves. He went through the customary motions and knelt down before looking underneath the door from the accustomed angle. Jimmy looked for the usual tell-tale signs, the chief of these being trousers without folds. Seeing trousers with folds he opened the door and admitted the waiting guards who stepped briskly into the back-yard with a view to entering the back kitchen where our customers were happily seated, engaged in soft conversation as they discussed the events of the previous days, national and local. Tones were hushed and no voice carried. In fact, it could be said that the exterior of a busy public house after hours when guards are about is quieter than a grave-yard at night.

'What's the meaning of this?' Jimmy asked as he drew himself to his full height of five feet, two inches.

The two civic guards were greatly taken aback and quite rightly, believing that it was they who should have been posing such a question and not Jimmy Jay.

'Explain yourself,' said Mike.

'Yes,' said Jerry, 'explain yourself.'

After they had spoken they pushed their caps back on their foreheads and spread their large feet as they awaited an explanation.

'Bad form,' said Jimmy, with all the righteousness he could muster.

'Dang it man,' said Jerry, 'we're only doing our job.'

'Doing your job,' said Jimmy truculently, 'with no trousers on!'

The pair looked downwards to reassure themselves that they had trousers on. They looked upwards into a much-improved starry sky, a Christmas sky before looking downwards again to confirm that their trousers were indeed on. Whiskey can play strange pranks even on policemen so they felt their trousers to be sure.

'We have trousers on,' they said in unison.

'Yes,' said Jimmy Jay, 'but not guards' trousers and that's not very sporting.'

'Not very sporting!' the minions of the law echoed incredulously.

'When I looked out under the door,' Jimmy Jay

informed them, 'I did not see trousers without folds so I admitted you in good faith, thinking you were ordinary folk like myself but what do I find, only two guards!'

Mike and Jerry explained that they had been engaged in some interior decorating all day and forgot to change into their on-duty trousers. They were most contrite and assured Jimmy that they would never involve themselves in such duplicity.

Did I say earlier that they had drunk the best part of a bottle of whiskey between them during their extra-curricular activities. The bottle had been a gift from Mike's wife. She stayed in the house until the painting and the wall-papering were completed, measuring out drops of the precious whiskey every time they seemed to flag or lose concentration.

'We're truly sorry Jimmy,' said Mike, 'because this not our style at all.'

'Yes,' said Jerry, 'truly sorry. It was bad form on our part and it is not our style at all as Mike says.'

'I'm glad to hear you say that,' said Jimmy Jay, 'it restores my faith in that wonderful body of men known as the garda síochána but I have to say that if tonight's visit was intentional then it was unsporting.'

'It was most unsporting,' said Mike who nudged Jerry with an elbow and was nudged back in return.

'Unsporting it was without doubt,' Jerry agreed, 'but we are now prepared to withdraw and let the matter rest.'

So grateful was Jimmy Jay that he invited the pair to have a pint. He was permitted such extravagances in the rarest of circumstances only. The guards declined on the grounds that they were a danger to shipping already.

'I'll tell you something now Jimmy,' said Mike, 'and it is this. I will never again raid a public house without a guards' trousers on me.'

'Me too,' said Jerry as they hurried home to don their lawful trousers.

One of the neighbours wrote a song about it in the air of 'The Great American Railway'. The exact words escape me just now but they went something like this:

> 'Twas the year of sixty-four
> Those outlaws bold fell in their gore
> He shot them down with his forty-four
> In the famous William Street showdown.
> The Kid stood his ground quite unafraid
> Saying 'Undertaker where's your spade?'
> Come take these boys to yonder glade
> From the famous William Street Showdown.

I remember that far-off morning as though it were yesterday. The crows had taken leave of the street's tall chimneys and sashayed westwards shortly after the peals of the nine o'clock bell announced the arrival of a watery sun.

'That sun sure don't look too good,' the crows seemed to caw to each other but then they were gone and the street assumed an eerie silence. It was a silence of a kind that the street had never experienced before and old folk who were abroad at the time would say later that it boded no good.

'Well cut my legs off and call me Shorty,' said one old timer, 'if there ain't a showdown o' some kind this mawnin'.'

'You reckon?' said his wife.

'I reckon,' came the studied response.

New Year's Eve would fall on the following day

and the William Streeters, no strangers to strong liquor, would celebrate and hold hands and sing 'Auld Lang Syne' and other sentimental songs until they could sing no more.

At approximately nine-thirty my four year old son Conor, resplendent in his new cowboy suit, appeared on the street. He pushed back his Stetson and took stock of his bailiwick.

Jim Carroll addressed his employer Stuart Stack who owned the Arcade next door: 'It's the William Street Kid,' he said in awe and hurriedly hung up the remainder of the coarse brushes before skedaddling indoors to safety.

'Howdy Kid,' said Stuart. He knew the Kid well and was sure he wouldn't shoot a neighbour. Then a dog barked from a nearby door-way and the Kid went for his gun.

'It's just a dawg,' Stuart spoke mollifyingly.

The William Street Kid returned the gun to its holster and went back indoors for his porridge.

Time passed. So did some overhead clouds and so did a mild drizzle and the watery sun reappeared but the sense of foreboding and the feeling of tension had intensified. A cat appeared, an indication that the neighbourhood dogs smelled trouble and decided to spend the morning in bed. Then it happened out of the blue.

A few elderly stragglers made their way homewards from nine o'clock Mass and out from the bowels of the post office, in full regalia, stepped Mick the Post. A rotund, dark-jowled individual in his late fifties, he did not escape the attention of the William Street Kid.

Mick the Post stood for a while on the pavement, sniffing the wind for rain, a common practice at the time. When he was satisfied that no rain was likely he tightened the strap of his bag and moved down the street.

Mick the Post, however, wasn't all that he seemed to be. To the elderly Mass folk he was their neighbourhood postman with nothing in his head but the safe delivery of his letters, especially the registered ones. The William Street Kid wasn't so easily duped. He recognised the hardened features of Black Bill the rustler under the official post office cap. The Kid's hands hovered over his guns, a steely look in his blue eyes, his legs apart, his body hunched forward. Black Bill saw the Kid almost at once. He stood stock still, his jowl set as he wetted his trigger fingers from his rapidly drying gums. He loosened his bag straps and allowed the post-bag to fall to the pavement. He did not go for his guns at once. His hand movements were fidgety. His body leaned from one side to the other. His facial muscles flickered and then he sang out that terrifying command that had petrified sheriffs and posses alike: 'Go for your gun!'

The Kid smiled wryly but made no move. Jim Carroll and his boss Stuart Stack held their coarse brushes close to their chests. The elderly slipped into the neighbourhood shops and waited for the trouble to blow over.

'Dang you, you mangy hound dog,' Black Bill was at it again, 'I won't tell you no more. Go for your gun!'

Still the Kid made no move.

'Go for yours,' he commanded in a tone free of emotion. Black Bill hesitated. The terror of a hundred cowtowns, with forty notches on his gun-handle, drew like lightning. One minute his hands were empty and the next they were filled with blazing guns. Fast as he was he wasn't as fast as the Kid. His move was faster than lightning. He didn't draw two guns. He drew one. He didn't shoot twelve times like Black Bill. He shot once. Black Bill clutched his breast. A despairing cry escaped his throat. The cry was made up of a gurgle, a groan and a grunt. He staggered up and he staggered down. He staggered hither and he staggered thither and then he fell to the ground on top of his saddle-bags.

'He's deader,' said Jim Carroll, 'than an Egyptian mummy.'

The William Street Kid relieved Jim and his boss of their coarse brushes. They surrendered them meekly. They promised never to use them again.

Later, well out into the day, there was a New Year spirit abroad. The four principals, the Kid, Jim Carroll, Stuart Stack and Mick the Post sat in the snug of these here licensed premises where they partook of some festive drinks. Mick the Post looked alive and well considering that he had been plugged only a few hours before. Then the snug door opened and Berkie Browne, the butcher, burst in.

'I need a posse fast,' he explained. The four comrades stood to attention after they had bolted their drinks.

'You guys promise to uphold the law?' Berkie Browne posed the question asked of many a brave cowboy before.

'We shorely do sheriff,' Jim Carroll spoke on behalf of his deputies. So the posse, led by their sheriff, headed south across the mesquite for Jet Carroll's pub where they made camp for the night.

Shortly afterwards the William Street Kid returned home. He hung up his guns and allowed himself to be tucked in.

'Where's yore podners?' I asked.

'My podners is a singin' round Jet's campfire,' he answered drowsily as he gently spurred his mount towards the horizon, beyond which lay the river of dreams and the Land of Nod where all small boys must go sooner or later.

THE WORD OF A WRENBOY

He lived in a lane-way close to our street. To say he was spare would be unfair to him. He was sparer than spare and he would be dapperer than dapper as well if only he had a decent suit. Despite this one could see that he was made to be dapper but was denied by circumstance. When I first knew him he was roughly seventy years of age although some said he was nearer to eighty. He survived on a modest subvention from the state and on the occasional gifts from friends and neighbours. His full name was Walter Aloysius Rogan but he was known locally as the Wrenboy Rogan.

All his life he had been an unpaid errand boy. Well maybe he wasn't altogether unpaid because everybody in the street gave him something for Christmas, a few shillings or even a pound, often a drink or a meal if it was going and he chanced to be in the vicinity. It was on the day of the wren or St Stephen's Day that he came into his own.

The traditional bands of wrenboys from the countryside within a radius of ten miles would appear sooner or later and march round the streets and squares, visiting pubs and soliciting from all those they chanced to meet. With the money gathered each group would host a wren dance before January blew itself out.

The Wrenboy Rogan did not belong to any group of wrenboys nor did he wear the traditional dress of the wrenboys nor did he proceed outwards into the countryside for fear of getting wet. When it rained or hailed or snowed he withdrew to the nearest tavern and beat gently on the toy tambourine which was really no more than a travesty of the great bodhráns or goatskin drums which authentic wrenboys always carried

The traditional wrenboys suffered the presence of the Wrenboy Rogan when it became apparent to them many years before that it was not his intent to traduce themselves or their venerated drums. Sooner or later before the day ended the toy tambourine would disappear. Generally it would be left behind in a pub but there had been times when neighbourhood black-guards would purloin it so that they might tease its owner when he emerged from a pub after the rain or the sleet had ceased.

When the Wrenboy Rogan demanded the return of his property all he received was abuse. Too drunk to apprehend the thief and too old to give chase after those who mocked him he would be obliged to sit on a window sill from where he would recount the be-smirched family ancestries and pauperised circum-stance of his persecutors-in-chief. The Wrenboy Rogan had a tongue harsher than driving hail and a genuine penchant for exposing the most sensitive areas of his enemies family cupboards. Some of his more blister-ing assessments had found a deserved place in the local top twenty of outstanding personal smears. When left alone he was a mild enough soul, well liked and even respected despite his obvious flaws. The problem lay in his merciless accuracy in the realms of revilement. He made enemies, enemies without the wit or vocal skills to reprimand him in kind. This left the enemies with no choice but to retaliate physically which they often did.

'It is truly an astonishing fact that professional boxers of my acquaintance,' Dr Matt Coumer confided to his friend Sergeant Ruttle, 'have assured me that there is no way a boxer could survive the Wrenboy Rogan beatings without being punch drunk or even dead.' They were seated at either side of the Wrenboy's bed in Trallock General Hospital on wrenboys' night. Earlier the Wrenboy had gone a taunt too far with the result that his victim, a disgraced amateur boxer, had given the Wrenboy the worst beating to which he had ever been subjected.

The amateur boxer had snatched the Wrenboy's toy tambourine from the hands of a less militant mischief-maker and danced on it. He then folded his arms and asked the Wrenboy what he proposed to do about it. Incapacitated by drink as he was the Wrenboy nevertheless rose to his feet and assumed a fighting pose.

'In a sober state,' Bill Ruttle was to say later, 'my money would be on the Wrenboy in spite of his years.' The sergeant had seen his fancy in several brawls but with a mixture of skill and sheer courage the Wrenboy had always come out on top. With drink inside him he looked and behaved like a boxing clown.

As he lay on the bed he winced when ever he was obliged to change his position. Despite his scarred face the Wrenboy was not in the least repulsive and, according to the sergeant, was never short of a girlfriend.

'He has a way with dogs, with children and with certain local damsels.'

'Excuse me,' the doctor cut across him, 'it goes beyond local damsels. My own wife says he's the most likeable rogue in town.'

'And so does mine,' Bill threw back. The friends sat together marvelling at the constitution of the veteran on the bed. Matt took the Wrenboy's wrist in his and shook his head.

'Bad?' Bill asked concernedly

'There are worse walking the streets,' the doctor informed the sergeant, 'but this man's problem is his age and, of course, his drinking. What happens now?'

'What happens now,' the sergeant responded, 'is that he'll follow the usual pattern. That is to say he'll depart this place some time tomorrow or after or as soon as his head clears. Then he'll lie up for a day or two. If you were to take up your position near his abode you could see the usual soft-hearted carers arriving in turns with cloth-covered trays and soup tureens and occasionally your favourite dessert and my favourite scones. He won't starve and that's for sure. He'll re-cuperate and put on a little fat on that skeletal frame of his and then as he's been doing for years he'll call to the presbytery and ask if our beloved parish priest, the Right Reverend Canon Cornelius Coodle is available. The housekeeper will look him up and down and ask him if he's hungry but he'll inform her in his own charming way that he is hungry not for food of the body but rather is he hungry for food of the soul. She will lead him without a word to the sitting-room and gently knock upon the door.

'"Who is it?" à drowsy voice will ask.

'"It is Mister Rogan to see you canon," Mrs Hanlon will call back.

'"Come!" the voice from within will call and so once more comes round the annual confrontation between the Wrenboy Rogan and Canon Cornelius Coodle.'

When Dr Coumer and Sergeant Ruttle left the district hospital they hit upon the idea that a visit to their favourite hostelry might not be amiss. So it was that they found themselves in the back room at Crutleys. After four pints of stout apiece they decided upon a few turns round the town square after which they gravitated naturally to the humble and deserted abode of the Wrenboy Rogan. They were surprised to see the open door and to hear the flurry of female feet as three unidentified women seized the opportunity in the Wrenboy's absence, to turn his dwelling-place inside out. All that could be seen from the lane-way outside were the forms of frantic females as they changed bed-clothes, washed ware, cleaned the fireplace and performed the countless other chores which can transform a house.

'Let's move,' Bill cautioned, 'before they find something for us to do.' The friends resumed their stroll. As they were about to pass by the grave-yard Matt suddenly stopped as though inspired by the nearness of the parish's faithful departed.

'We both know,' Matt looked absently at the Celtic Crosses and lesser monuments, 'that the Wrenboy is headed for this very spot if he breaks out again.'

'Well I don't know,' Bill spoke hesitantly, 'but I'll

take your word for it if you say so.'

'It's odds on,' the doctor assured him, 'there will be a coma and then the heart will fail and that will be that.'

'And if he doesn't break out?'

'If he doesn't break out he could enjoy a few more years, that is if life can really be enjoyed without booze. Still, it would be my opinion that he could have a few worthwhile years without the drink. It's just a matter of putting his mind to it.'

'You really think he'll fall by the wayside again?' the sergeant asked.

'It's his choice,' was all Matt would contribute by way of answer.

A surge of loneliness unexpectedly overcame the sergeant. He recalled a night when he was new to the division and bit off more than he could chew. He was put the pin of his collar to defend himself against three blackguards who had assaulted him when the town was asleep. Apparently they had become incensed at the sight of the uniform. Then the one calamity that he feared most overcame him when he accidentally slipped and fell to the ground. It was at that precise moment that the Wrenboy Rogan appeared. With flailing boots and fists he shocked the blackguards with the fury of his assault. Add to this the blood-curdling whoops that surely belonged to some inhuman creature from the grave-yard nearby.

It was just the opening the sergeant needed so desperately. Between them the lawman and his deputy apprehended the blackguards and left them with painful posteriors for many a day afterwards. A bond developed between the two men. Chapter by chapter over the years the Wrenboy unfolded the sorry saga of his life from the awful day in his early twenties when his wife ran away with another man. He had come to the town where he now resided from the east of the country. He had been a roustabout with a circus but had lost his job for repeated drunkenness.

'I've been proceeding backwards all my life,' he told Bill, 'and that's the story of my life.

'If any man can get him to go off the juice, you're that man.' Matt's waters flowed freely against the graveyard wall. 'He respects you more than any man in town. If you were to ask him to give you his word that he would abstain from the drink for good he might just do it.' Matt tied his flies and looked up at the sickle moon. 'Do you notice a preponderance of sickle moons lately,' he asked, 'or is it my imagination?'

'Too much drink,' his friend replied.

'You mean too little drink,' Matt countered.

'What brings you friend?' Canon Coodle asked as the Wrenboy stood abashed with bent head and trembling hands. It occurred to the canon that he had been asking the very same question since his first annual meeting with the parish's most distinguished drunkard.

'I've come to take the pledge canon,' the Wrenboy opened. It was exactly what the canon expected because every year since his appointment to the parish the Wrenboy had arrived unfailingly a few days after the beginning of the new year and announced that he wished to take the pledge. Each year he seemed to be more forlorn and more emaciated.

'If the pledge is what you want,' the canon said resignedly, 'the pledge it shall be.'

Immediately the Wrenboy went on his knees and made the sign of the cross. Neither was strictly required but the canon felt that they added dignity to the occasion and should not be discouraged.

'For how long this time?' the canon asked, the resignation still unmistakable in his voice.

'For life,' came the terse reply.

'For life!' the canon wanted to make sure he heard right.

'For life!' from the Wrenboy.

'Now,' said the canon planting his long legs apart and folding his arms to show that he was not taking the request lightly, 'you have been coming here for as long as I can remember and on each occasion you have taken the pledge for life. My sources tell me that far from taking the pledge for life all you seem to be able to manage is a week or two and on occasion you broke all records by going off it for a month when you had pneumonia.'

'It's different this time,' the Wrenboy Rogan assured his parish priest. 'This time I mean it.'

The Wrenboy allowed his hand to gingerly touch his badly scared face. He placed his index finger on the most recent acquisition to the many eloquent disfigurations which covered his countenance from ear to ear.

'I can't take anymore of these,' he told the canon, 'so you see it has to be for life this time'

'Maybe you're being too hard on yourself,' the canon placed a wooden crucifix in the applicant's hands, 'nobody would think any the worse of you if you tried it for six months or a year or, better still, until the first day of Trallock Races. That would give your stomach a chance to settle and your mental outlook could only improve as well. It's just a little over eight months away and you would also have the satisfaction that you kept your bond with your saviour and with yourself.'

'No canon,' the Wrenboy was adamant. 'It has to be for life.'

'You're the boss,' Canon Coodle told him.

'All you have to do now is promise that you will never touch another drink for the remainder of your natural life.'

The canon was beginning to enjoy himself. He particularly savoured the determined features and the grim mouth, the closed eyes and the head bent in supplication as the tears of remorse began to flow and the torrent of aspirations as the hands tightened on the crucifix.

'I promise,' the Wrenboy sobbed ,'never to touch another drink for the remainder of my natural life.'

'With the help of God now you'll be able to change your ways,' the canon helped him to his feet, 'a bit of resolve is all you need.'

'Would you hear my confession canon while you're at it? I'd like to be in the state of grace starting out.'

Donning his stole the canon indicated a chair near the canonical armchair and turned his head towards the penitent. He listened without change of expression and, as always with the Wrenboy, the canon felt reassured and in some ways consoled by the humility and the innate goodness of the misfit beside him.

'There but for the grace of God' the canon told himself after he had dispensed forgiveness and imposed a simple penance. Canon Coodle accompanied the shrivelled Wrenboy to the presbytery entrance where they shook hands and wished each other well.

The days after Christmas stretched themselves imperceptibly and old people would say to each other 'there is a cock's step after coming into the days'. The saying was a relic from the Gaelic and the more scholars dwelt on it the more valid it seemed to be. The strutting cock had a very high, and therefore a very, short step. It would be several days before the stretch in the afternoons became noticeable.

In the estuary the first salmon began to show themselves before moving upriver and the lapwings, birds of the five names as they were called locally, began to break up into smaller flocks preparatory to mating. The names were lapwing, green plover, crested plover, peewit and pilibeen. The last were two Gaelic names resembling the cries of the bird in question depending on how skilled the human interpretation might be. Showers of hail became more common and there were flurries of snow but by and large it was a moderate winter. Snowdrops brightened the sheltered areas and there were signs that the more adventurous of the daffodils would bloom in the weeks ahead. All in all there were ample signs that spring was just around the corner.

Then on the fourth day of the new season, thirty-two days after he had taken the pledge for life, Walter Aloysius Rogan went back on the booze. Word spread quickly and those who always said so said 'I knew it would happen any day now.' He had managed to save a sizeable part of his dole money and, because he had been well fed and well looked after during his sojourn in the world of sobriety, he made an all-out assault on liquor for three days which saw him stretched on the third night under the blind eye of Trallock Bridge in a state of semi-consciousness. Nobody ever found out how he got there. None could recall having seen him in the vicinity of the bridge and the Wrenboy himself had no recollection whatsoever. When he was discovered by two salmon poachers they firmly believed that he was dead but when they dragged him to high ground they heard the moans which told them that he was still in the land of the living.

When the Wrenboy opened his eyes in a bed in Trallock District Hospital the first face he saw was that of Canon Cornelius Coodle.

'The last time I saw you I gave you the pledge,' the canon told him, 'and just now I've anointed you. What have you to say for yourself at all you unfortunate creature?'

'Drink, canon,' the Wrenboy replied before he closed his eyes to sleep as he had never slept before.

The Wrenboy spent several days recuperating. Not once did he speak of the events which very nearly led to his demise under the blind eye of the bridge where at least two errant drunkards had died from exposure within living memory. For hours at a time he had padded round the hospital in a pair of new bedroom slippers bought for him by the epic poet Mental Nossery. They were the first bedroom slippers he ever owned. When he believed that his full health had returned to him he made his plans. After counting his remaining money he came to the conclusion that he had sufficient for a comprehensive two-day booze. The Wrenboy counted his resources in drinks. His dole money for instance, after a few minor items such as food and electricity were deducted, amounted to six half whiskeys and eleven pints of stout with the price of a box or two of matches left over.

On the day of his departure from Trallock District Hospital he was visited by Sergeant Bill Ruttle who asked for a personal favour.

'I won't put a tooth in it,' Bill Ruttle opened, 'I have come here to see you for one reason only and that is to ask you for a personal favour.'

'I'll do anything for you,' the Wrenboy promised.

'Will you go off the drink for me?'Bill asked.

'That's a different story,' the Wrenboy's face grew serious.

'Will you or won't you go off the drink for me?'

'I could try,' from the Wrenboy.

'That's not good enough,' the sergeant told him.

'What's gotten into you?' the Wrenboy asked while he studied his friend's face.

'Nothing's gotten into me,' the sergeant looked out the widow into the bleak afternoon beyond.

'You really want me to go off the drink on a permanent basis?'

'What I really want,' the sergeant turned on him, 'is to see you hold on to your life for a few more years.'

'I'll take the pledge,' the Wrenboy volunteered.

'No you won't,' Bill Ruttle injected a new inflexi-bility into his tone. 'I am asking you to give me your word as a gentleman that you will never put an intoxi-cating drink to your lips again.'

'I am not a gentleman,' came the evasive reply.

'Then,' said Bill, 'I'm asking you on the word of a man.'

'I'm not much of a man,' came the equally evasive reply.

'I'm beginning to see that,' the sergeant obser-ved angrily.

A silence followed. It was that kind of silence where the wrong word could bring negotiations to an immediate end.

'All right,' Bill was now using a more reasonable tone, 'I'm asking you on the word of a wrenboy.'

There would be no evasion this time and Bill knew it. The sounds from the nearby corridors and wards became more pronounced as the silence bet-ween the two men became more pronounced. The Wrenboy sat on the side of the bed on which he had been lying and covered his face with his hands. He felt like saying to his friend that what was being asked was grossly unfair, that it was totally impossible, that it was not in his capacity or character to make such a promise, that he just didn't have the will power. In-stead he said nothing at all. He just sat there looking at Bill's beefy side-face. Then he rose and took his friend's hand. As he shook it he spoke: 'On the world of a wrenboy,' he said.

No other words passed between them at that

time but Bill Ruttle said many years later as he and Matt Coumer looked down at the coffin of Walter Aloysius Rogan, that a wrenboy's word was his bond.

A Christmas Surprise

Masterman sipped his whiskey elegantly knowing that he was being watched by the tall grey-haired lady who had just entered the hotel's plush bar. He noticed her earlier in the foyer and, from her easy air of proprietorship, guessed that she was a member of the staff.

More than likely she was a supervisor of some sort. It wouldn't surprise him if she turned out to be the manageress. He guessed she would be in her mid-fifties. While she continued to take stock of him he produced a spotless white handkerchief from the breast pocket of his second-best suit. He did not blow his nose. He never did so publicly. Rather did he remove some non-existent specks from the sleeves of his coat.

She was moving about now, outside the counter, but at the far end of the bar. The barmaid followed her to the outside and rang the Waterford glass time-up bell which she carried in her hand. The older woman left the bar, stately as a sailing ship and erect as any mast.

Masterman noted the trim figure and especially the way her buttocks flickered tantalisingly as she passed by. She favoured him with the barest of nods as though nods were at a premium at that time. Then she paused briefly and with a hint of a smile informed him in low-tones that he was to ignore the bell and stay where he was until she returned. He nodded eagerly and looked at his watch. In a mere ten minutes it would be Christmas Day, the twenty-eight such day he had spent in a world which, he felt, still owed him something substantial for his years of sexual frustration and general all round suffering.

He might have married but on the two occasions where matters had taken a turn towards permanence he had withdrawn from the relationships. His sister had married and was coming home for Christmas. The reason he found himself in the hotel on Christmas Eve was due to the fact that his in-laws, notably his brother-in-law, a despicable wretch perverted and mean, were spending Christmas in the family home where he himself had spent the previous twenty-seven Christmases. The hotel he had chosen attracted him for two reasons. Firstly it was at the opposite end of the country to his family home and secondly the rates were more than reasonable for the Christmas period. His in-laws would be departing the family home on the day after St Stephen's Day and this would give him the opportunity to spend a day with his parents.

His thoughts returned to the hotel manageress who, he had by now deduced, she undoubtedly must be. He looked at his watch. Half-past twelve. Over a half-hour had passed since she intimated that she would be returning. No sign of her. Customers had been vacating the bar on a regular basis in the interim, wishing each other the compliments of the season. None had over-looked him as they exited. All had extended to him Christmas greetings and he had dutifully responded.

At last the bar was emptied and he turned his thoughts for a second time to the manageress, sophisticated and mature without doubt and immaculately preserved to boot, he imagined she would have a lot to offer if the mood caught her but, of course, she could have asked him to stay for any number of reasons.

He had heard from other commercials that women of her ilk and age were at the top of the scale, skilled, practised, discreet and totally abandoned once they had committed themselves.

Masterman recalled similar females he had encountered in his travels. He had been singularly unsuccessful in engaging the attention of a solitary one. In fact he had found them gruff and even surly when they discovered what was on his mind. Why then, he asked himself, should this particular one ask him to remain behind until she returned?

He looked at his watch a second time and then he drifted into a deep sleep induced unexpectedly by the hundreds of miles he had travelled that day and by the countless whiskeys he had drunk.

In his sleep he dreamed of far-off days when youth held little care. He dreamed of the same dark-haired nymph who led him countless merry dances through radiant summer scenes and when he woke up several hours later he found himself looking into cold grey eyes set in beautiful, if rather severe, features.

He closed his eyes temporarily to make sure that the visage over-looking him was not part of the dream sequence he had just experienced. When he re-opened his eyes the over-hanging face was still there. The rich red lips which were the outstanding feature of the face opened and from there issued forth a soft vocal chain of apology. She had meant to return but had fallen asleep herself explaining that she had spent seventeen hours on her feet throughout Christmas Eve. Would he forgive her and join her for breakfast in the dining-room? She took him gently by the hand lest he refuse and led him into a corner where a smart young waitress with a beaming smile awaited their instructions.

Full Irish for two and no frills. As they waited he observed that her lips were impeccably lip-sticked but that she wore no other make-up. There was about her a crispness and a freshness which he had never before encountered in a female. It was as if she had spent the preceding hours at nothing else but immersing herself in fragrant waters, drying herself and re-immersing herself until her full vigour had been restored.

The lights of the dining-room shone brightly for it was still dark outside but she shone brighter albeit in a different way.

'I had the night porter keep an eye on you,' she confided, 'can you guess how long you've been sleeping?'

He shook his head for it was not in his power to produce a spoken reply. He was, as he was to confide afterwards to a fellow-commercial, in a trance. 'I felt,' he had said at the time, 'like one of those romantic Gaelic poets who has been discovered in the wilderness by a beautiful goddess in the dead of night.'

The woman who sat opposite him at the table was now in full vocal spate, had been widowed some ten years before, heart attack, no children, lived presently with her sister and doting husband and three young children, four, six and eight, the younger, girls, the oldest a boy. Dream kids all, fun loving and sweet.

When breakfast arrived she ceased talking for a moment in order to pour the scalding tea. As he wolfed down his food she proceeded with her life's tale. Now in her early fifties she had never considered re-marrying. She had found happiness with her sister and her family. She had resumed her hotel career a few short weeks after her husband's death and this had been a blessing in that she worked herself into total exhaustion every day and night so that sleep presented no problem and she didn't have time for self-pity.

Promotion followed and she was now the hotel's manageress. As she spoke she reminded him some-times of a nun, sometimes of a school-mistress, some-times of a madame and occasionally of a sergeant-major. There was no denying one important factor however. She was still a beautifully preserved woman.

'You must have noticed that I spent more time than I should watching you in the bar last night,' she told him coyly. Before he could answer she explained that she had good reason. She went on to tell him that she would not go into it there and then.

'All will be revealed,' she assured him, 'and I pro-mise you will be pleased and fulfilled.'

It was the language that baffled Masterman. It had religious undertones when it shouldn't. Then he reminded himself of commercial tales about prim, prudish women who exceeded themselves when the chips were down, unbelievable tales but authentic as any tale could be and verified by the fathers of com-mercial rooms up and down the country ever since sales representatives forgathered to exchange business experiences and gripping yarns of sweet romance.

'Now,' she said with finality as she looked at her watch, 'it's twenty minutes to eight and,' here she paused briefly, 'at ten minutes to the hour we will leave here and hasten to the church which happens to be just around the corner.'

Before he could utter a single word she placed a finger firmly on his lips and cautioned him to silence. 'Speak not,' she whispered fervently as she looked into his rather bloodshot eyes. 'Speak not,' she begged, 'or my dream will fade.'

Masterman submitted himself once more to the trance world he had occupied earlier. Dutifully he followed her and found himself shortly afterwards seated in the very front pew of the church ablaze with light and reverently hymnal all around.

Masterman, if he was asked by a colleague, would admit that he hadn't seen the inside of a church since his sister's wedding ten years before.

When Mass was over they returned to the hotel and in the foyer she faced him with a strange revelation.

'I'm asking you to do something for me now,' she said, 'and afterwards there won't be a single word to anybody. It will be our secret.'

Masterman nodded eagerly and did not object when she took him by the hand and led him upstairs to the door-way of his very own bedroom.

Masterman's astonishment did not show on his face. It would never do, he told himself, to behave as if such a thing never happened before. She handed him the key which she had earlier collected at reception. It was she who led the way into the room where, immediately, he endeavoured to place his trembling hands around her.

'Patience,' she admonished. He dropped his hands to his sides.

'Now,' she spoke curtly, 'take off your coat and your shirt and I'll be back in a minute.' So saying she lifted the key from the bed where he had flung it and vacated the room.

Masterman sat baffled on the side of the bed which he hoped to utilise to its fullest before the morning took its course. Without further reflection he jumped to his feet. First things first, he told himself. He would do as she had told him. Off would come coat and shirt and he would await further instructions. When the door opened after a gentle preliminary knock she entered bearing a large plastic bag. From it she withdrew a tasselled, crimson Santa Claus hat and an equally crimson, outsized Santa Claus coat.

'Now,' she said with her sergeant-major voice, 'get these on you and we'll head for my sister's.'